# Puttin' On the Dog & Gettin' Bit!

## Infamous Family Fables, Feuds,
## and Festivities from My Life

# Barbara Taylor Sanders

Express Image Publications

Barbara Taylor Sanders can be contacted at:
expressimagepublications@gmail.com
www.barbarataylorsanders.com

First printing, October 2018
© October 2018 Barbara Taylor Sanders
Also available on eBook with Kindle Digital Publishing

ISBN: 9781726838092

# Puttin' On the Dog & Gettin' Bit
## A Memoir of Sorts

# Publications by
# Barbara Taylor Sanders

Non-Fiction

*The Laborer's Are Few (Father's Press, 2011)*
*Holy Spirit: For Real*

Fiction

*Bloodline Secrets*
*The Bloodstone Ring*
*More Than A Promise*

# Dedicated to

My dearest mother, Shirley Ann, who is the funniest person I know. As a teenager, I loved sharing a hearty laugh whenever you read something especially funny from Erma Bombeck's newspaper column.

Thank you for your priceless gift of humor, Mom. In spite of all you've been through with your stroke, we can still find something to chuckle about, can't we?

# In Loving Memory

Lydia Margaret Brant, my great-grandmother, who passed her delightful sense of humor down a long line of family members who love to cut up and have fun. Her gift of hospitality remains strong among us as well, known as "the Indian way."

Elsie Aldean Brant Lambert, my grandmother, who died too young at the age of 49. Suffering Rheumatic fever at a young age that weakened her heart with a risk for childbirth. Thank you for sacrificing your life to home-birth the seven surviving children out of the nine babies you carried in your short life. We cherish your bravery and love of life.

Catherine "Katie" Lambert Fishman, my dear aunt who often shared the brighter side of life through her hilarious stories.

Dr. Richard Steit, my comic relief! Oh, how I enjoyed cutting up with you and Laurie, during some very special, light-hearted times in Centerville, Ohio. Sadly, we also lost Laurie this past year.

Lori Snow, for your gift of humor, encouragement, inspiration and excellence in our weekly fiction-writing critique group.

"A cheerful disposition is good for your health;
Gloom and doom leave you bone-tired."

Proverbs 17:22 (The Message Bible)

# Table of Contents

# Puttin' On the Dog & Gettin' Bit

Whenever we have a cookout with friends, something always goes wrong. When first married, my husband and I had our biggest fights over something he forgot to do. It's a wonder we're still married after all these decades. For instance, the coals on the barbeque grill. It was Daryl's only job, and we always ended up waiting another thirty minutes till the charcoal was hot enough to grill the meat.

My late Aunt Katie commiserated about Uncle Herm, and the infamous time when three neighborhood couples came for what was supposed to be an elegant sit-down dinner.

During the preceding week, Katie, an immaculate housekeeper, still cleaned out closets and drawers, scrubbed down walls, wallpapered a bathroom, swept out the garage, trimmed bushes, mowed the lawn, planted flowers, painted the front door, washed and re-hung curtains, decorated, cleaned silverware, and shopped for food, candles, and mauve linen napkins. Nothing like "company coming" to get you motivated! Completely exhausted by the day of the dinner party, she managed to bake, cook and set an elegant table for the grand finale. It was perfect except for one thing. She left a simple, lone task to her husband.

The big evening arrived. The four couples were seated in a romantic, candlelight setting. The dimly lit dining table was adorned with fresh pink flowers and coordinating starched and ironed linens. Each silver-rimmed plate awaited the grand arrival of skewered shish kabobs on a large platter, fresh out of the broiler. My aunt confidently jumped into action. It was her finest moment. All eyes were transfixed on the presentation as she swiftly slid grilled steak and vegetables off each skewer to tower on a mound of piping hot, perfectly fluffed, white rice. With the precision of a Sous Chef, it came together like a fine-tuned symphony.

The dish looked and smelled divine. The hungry guests were ready to dig right in. My smiling auntie gracefully sat down and gently nodded to my Uncle Herm, seated at the head of the table. She waved her arm, gesturing like a master conductor toward the guy with a set of huge cymbals. She had placed him in charge of purchasing the wine, opening the bottle, filling the glasses, then making a special toast to good food and wonderful friends. That moment never happened.

He lifted the wine bottle to pour.

"So, Kate? Where's the cork screw opener?"

Undaunted, my aunt rushed back to the kitchen. The dinner guests could hear her yanking open drawer after drawer to no avail. It seemed like she was gone for twenty minutes. Jumping up, one man piped, "Oh, I'll run next door and get ours." All three men leaped to their feet on cue and rushed out together as if the house was on fire. They disappeared for a true twenty-minutes. I would have hated to be one of the guest wives waiting for their return. It probably felt like a medical lounge waiting for the results of a biopsy or facing a dreaded root canal.

Years later, we could laugh about it, but at the time Auntie Katie felt like skewering her husband. I know the feeling.

Through similar mishaps, I've learned that whenever you try *"puttin' on the dog, you end up gettin' bit!"*

# Charred Chicken Breasts, Anyone?

Many years ago, *Gourmet* magazine featured an amazing glazed chicken arrangement on its June cover. It motivated me to invite friends for a 4th of July cookout, to try this complicated recipe and show off my advanced culinary skills.

To save money, I skinned and de-boned ten whole-chicken breasts. The exotic recipe called for expensive spices I'd never heard of, so I bought them across town in a specialty shop. The three separate sauces were prepared and cooked in advance. One cooked-down sauce was marinade for the chicken, one sauce was to glaze while slow cooking, and another sauce was to pass after the chicken was roasted to a golden brown. In addition, the breasts were stuffed with a minced pecan mixture and wrapped in bacon – a time-consuming preparation. If you count the de-boning, three-made-from-scratch sauces and the two-hour drive time to buy the expensive, exotic spices, I spent about fifteen hours on this lone chicken recipe.

On the day of the cookout with friends, not leaving anything to chance, knowing my husband wouldn't have the coals just right, I took matters in my own hands. I fired up the coals in the outside grill about two hours before our guests arrived.

My "crowning moment" was to be the glorious honey-glazed chicken on the cover of Gourmet Magazine. As we were ready to dine, Susan was standing next to me, tossing the salad. We were elbow-to-elbow at my kitchen island as I sliced up hot garlic bread with a very long, sharp, pointed knife. My husband was outside with the other two men, grilling the glorious marinated chicken breasts.

Suddenly, my husband barged back into the kitchen, talking in a shaky, odd voice. Outstretched from his arms was the large white platter of chicken that I envisioned would look exactly like the June cover of *Gourmet* Magazine.

"You won't believe this," he began with eyeballs bulging. "You can ask the guys if you don't believe me – honest to God, all I did was put the lid down for thirty-seconds! When I opened it back up, the chicken looked like this!" His face was flushed from trying to explain

He cautiously set the dish of grilled chicken on the counter in front of Susan and me. Every single, delicately bacon-wrapped chicken breast had been singed to a coal black ball of tar-like matter. The platter was adorned with what looked like an ensemble of chard charcoal briquettes.

My legs buckled. I gasped. I managed to suppress my urge to stab him with the long, pointed knife, which had remained in stunned midair, suspension. I had a swoping desire to flee the room in tears to force our guests to vacate. My jaw dropped. Those sweeping, surges of emotions took my breath away and left me completely frozen. Susan broke the ice.

Leaning to my ear with a singsong voice, Susan whispered, "You know – the first one to forgive will get the blessing!"

I nearly turned the pointed, garlic bread-cutting knife on her.

Once we scraped the crusted chard off, the juicy chicken was cooked well enough to consume. My huge regret was not taking a picture of the blackened dainties to send to the editors of *Gourmet Magazine* for the cover of their August issue!

The humbling, bumbling, burnt chicken mishap created an atmosphere of true confessions from the wives. Donna piped up with a nightmare trying to impress her new neighbors with her pie-baking ability. One inspired summer day she drove out to a U-Pick-fruit farm in the country and picked two quarts of strawberries, one-by-one. That same day, pie dough was prepared with real butter, chilled, then artfully rolled out to fit in a brand new, over-sized, expensive Pyrex glass pie pan. The shell was baked and cooled, then filled with a yummy strawberry mixture made from the finest of ingredients.

The following day, Donna proudly presented the gorgeous pie with a "welcome-to-the-neighborhood" note, painstakingly written in calligraphy. The new neighbor, an absent-minded gynecologist, opened the front door to her smiling face. He reached out for the dazzling strawberry pie, thanked her, and then closed the door. Unfortunately, she never saw the white of the eyes of the little-lady residing in the home.

About five weeks later, Donna bumped in to one of their teenagers on the pathway leading to the lake. She greeted him with a friendly smile. "Hey, how did everyone enjoy the strawberry pie I made?" she grinned, expecting a gushing praise report.

"Oh, was that from *you?*" He frowned and scratched his head before confessing. "Yesterday, Mom was cleaning out the fridge and found it way in the back. It really grossed her out 'cuz it was completely covered with black mold. She just pitched the whole thing in the trashcan, pie plate and all. She wondered where it came from," he added with a chuckle before wandering off.

Hearing that story, Susan seized the chance to get something off her chest.

"Well, that reminds *me* of the time I brought over my homemade cherry strudel and it landed in *your* trashcan!" Her eyes were ablaze glaring at me.

I sneaked a peek at my husband. He shrugged his shoulders. We both drew blanks, which only added insult to injury.

"Cherry strudel?" I smiled weakly, completely dumbfounded.

"How could you *not* remember?" Her bright hazel eyes were still aflame. "It was Labor Day weekend, three years ago. I spent *all day* Friday making two large pans of cherry strudel. I brought the platters over on Saturday morning for your party on Monday. Remember how I told you, 'Now, this dessert, you can all eat right now, but don't let anyone touch this second platter. It's for Monday.' But, my cherry strudel was missing at your party. Since I didn't save any strudel for us – I was really looking forward to having some…Remember? When I asked where it was, you said, 'Oh, Daryl and the kids started digging in to it with spoons. It got real gooey and messy in the pan, so I just threw it out.' Then you went digging around in the trash can and found the remains in the aluminum foil."

Her eyes were still blazing, so I knew better then to sing, "The first to forgive—gets the blessing!"

During that jarring journey down memory lane, I deeply regretted not just schlepping a supermarket brand of cheap barbeque sauce over the chicken on my husband's ever loving, slow-start grill. So-what if we had to wait another half hour for the coals to be ready? It would have been just as tasty. But then again, I wouldn't have heard Susan's need for therapy because her glorious cherry strudel came up missing from my buffet table, *three-years* earlier!

I'm finally learning that whenever you try to *put on the dog, you always get bit!*

# Married to A Party Pooper

"Do I really have to go?" groaned my husband, not looking up from his computer. I sighed before appealing. I had expected resistance from him. After all, the Saturday late afternoon wedding reception was for a friend's son, whom he had never met.

"We don't have to stay that long, but we really do need to go," I gently coaxed.

From that point on my husband began to sulk, which gradually grew into an all-out stew. Although I chose to ignore his sullen mood, his curt remarks to me during the next few hours stung. Was I expecting too much?

This subtle form of animosity used to kindle feelings of guilt within me, igniting sparks between us. However, after thirty plus years of marriage, I no longer give in to manipulation. I have found a freedom worth sharing.

"I wonder what makes me detest going to these things so much?" asked Daryl pensively, as we pulled out of the driveway. He slowly drove down the street as if he were facing the guillotine.

"Yeah, I wonder, too. Why do you think?" I gently probed, hoping for some healthy dialogue about this age-old dilemma. Throughout the years, we would usually be so angry on the way to a social engagement, we'd drive along in hostile silence.

"I don't know…" He shrugged, with an air of indifference. We drove for a few more minutes before the oyster opened again.

"Maybe it's because I don't know what I could possible give to or get from these situations, but this of course, is not necessarily true."

Do all party poopers feel this way? I wondered.

It was keen insight, and I appreciated his candor. My dear husband was born with a melancholy temperament. I have learned to respect his reserve in social situations, knowing he'd rather be alone on an island reading a spy novel.

At social gatherings, he'll always be found in a corner making idle conversation with another loner, looking ill at ease and anxious to escape. I have learned to avoid getting "the eye" toward the door when I am having fun talking with friends. During the holidays with our extended family, Uncle Daryl will likely be found on the sideline playing cards in semi-silence in a sullen, four-some with similar dispositions.

I am at least thankful that my reluctant, but amiable, husband still goes out with me as a loving companion. He will never change, so I cannot cajole him into being the life-of-the-party. He has too many other wonderful qualities for me to be hung up on his lack of social graces. Besides, I enjoy being the life of the party.

Many years ago, on our way into a restaurant with a group of Dayton friends, I overheard a friend threaten her first-husband with divorce if he didn't talk during dinner. I certainly can relate, although once I get my husband out of the house, he usually comes alive. Getting my husband out has always been my greatest challenge. On the way home from the dreaded wedding reception, I looked over at him and lovingly patted his arm.

"Well, Mr. Social Butterfly, how'd you do back there?"

"Well, I survived," he said, sighing. "It was pure torture... exactly as I expected it to be...."

I smiled, shaking my head. I just had to ask, didn't I?

# Cut to the Chase!

A Few decades ago I recall watching TV with our son, Bo, who was home from college during spring break. When I asked him to hand me the remote control he looked genuinely amazed. "You're joking, right?"

Remote controls must be a male-dominated phenomenon because my husband, Daryl, acts the same way. However, now we each have our own television set in separate domains, so there is less friction between us.

Tonight, Daryl wandered into his man cave where I had been watching something on his big screen television. He suggested we watch a "saved" movie together. Oh the joys of T-VO! Whoever invented this brilliant recording device deserves the Nobel Prize. We can now race through commercials on two speeds...medium and fast forward.

Since I had been watching some other program, the remote was still in my possession. In our house we call it a "clicker" for short. I scrolled through the list of saved movies and began erasing those we'd already seen. The only movie we hadn't viewed yet was rated $1^{1/2}$ stars, a 1981 espionage flick.

"Hand me the clicker," commanded my husband in an authoritative tone. Without a word I surrendered my temporary power.

As the movie began playing, the credits were coming on the screen every few seconds. Daryl began fast-forwarding. Then an actor's lips moved, so he stopped to hear the spoken words. But after the dialogue exchange, my husband began fast-forwarding again to the next dialogue scene. When I protested, he became indignant as if his Reader's Digest version was the only way to watch a movie these days!

It was so absurd that I started laughing. "What?" he replied defensively, poker faced, annoyed that I had challenged him.

"I'm writing this one up for my book!" I snickered.

Another thing my dear hubby does is flick back and forth between two television programs, sometimes three. I've often come in the den to visit, unaware that he's engaged in two police detective series such as NCI and Law & Order, switching back and forth during commercial breaks. Or he'll check the scores on a few college football games, the NFL or the NBA, whenever the commercials coincide. I'll just start to fall into the story line of one show then wonder why it doesn't make sense, not realizing he's flicked over to the other program. It drives me nuts. Needless to say, we rarely ever watch television together.

When the remote is in your hand flashing through channels, the brain's capacity to compute everything whizzing along on the screen is amazing. However, if another person is the fast-moving data on the screen, it is too fast to comprehend. My husband will often yell, "Slow down!" as I am fast-forwarding channel selections with the remote. It's the same with me if he's rapidly scrolling through program titles.

We had an American missionary family visit us one weekend during their fund-raising furlough from China. Pastor

Dennis Balcombe is amazingly fluent in both Mandarin and Cantonese. His brother is a rocket scientist, so brains run in the family. One-night, while munching down a bag of chocolate-chip cookies, Pastor Dennis was clicking through the television channels at lightning speed. It was hilarious and such a guy-thing. It was then that I realized that even male missionaries aren't exempt from remote control domination.

I'm wondering what would happen if I seized possession of the TV remote during a saved, sacred segment of the NBA playoffs? Just imagine if I fast-forwarded until a hoop shot was made, then fast-forwarded to the next basketball score? Or what if I fast-forwarded during a pre-taped NFL game to just the plays when the football was passed from the quarterback, then fast-forwarded to the next down? Or better yet, when my husband takes a bathroom break during halftime, I fast-forward to the very end of the ball game to gleefully announce which team had won the game! After all, these days, don't we want to save time and just cut to the chase?

Just this week, Daryl grew weary of OSU getting slaughtered in a championship playoff, so he went to bed during the fourth quarter conceding defeat. I pay so little to football that I don't even know the opposing team to name it here. Daryl was taping the game in the man cave to finish watching during breakfast. Our son was back there, composing music while watching the game, but unbeknown to me, the game was about 20 minutes delayed from pausing for numerous snack or bathroom breaks.

On my TV in the living room, the late-night news commentator announced the stunning victory. Ohio State University was the winner! I quickly peeked in the bedroom to announce the exciting news, but Daryl was sound asleep. When I went back to share the joy with Bo, he said, "THANKS A LOT, Mom…. I'm not there yet!"

I glanced at the TV to see the game in full swing with the opposing team in the lead. That last minute O.S.U. touchdown must have been really exciting! So much for the one and only time I got engaged in a football game.

# Goodwill Misgivings

A few years back, my friend Susan got the not so bright idea to volunteer as "the cook" for her husband's annual trip to Belize (formerly British Honduras). Susan is the author of a bestselling cookbook and loves to entertain. This innocent invitation was a natural extension of her sizable gift of hospitality.

Don is a physician and one of the directors at a large medical clinic in Columbus, Ohio. For the past fifteen years "Doc" has organized goodwill medical trips to this impoverished country. His dedicated team of fellow volunteer doctors and nurses take donated medical supplies for about ten days of exhaustive, free-clinic service to the needy.

For months before Susan's first and last trip to Baize, she enthusiastically emailed family and friends, rounding up delicious recipes to whip up to feed the entire mission team. She specifically asked me for a delicious breakfast soufflé made with browned sausage, which I have often served for company Sunday brunch. She carefully packed the sausage in dry ice and hand carried it on the airplane across the ocean for a breakfast debut.

Doc failed to enlighten his wife, a glamorous redhead, about the hazards and hellish living conditions for the natives in that country. At the mission compound, the dilapidated kitchen was ill equipped. Fortunately, a fellow team member, who had been in that kitchen on a previous trip, taught Susan to ward off rats by banging dishpans on the exposed water pipes running down the kitchen wall. Since Susan and Don once served as medical director in India, living in an orphanage, she wasn't as traumatized by the sight of a rodent.

Her husband's energetic medical team rushed off early each morning, passing up a big breakfast because the tropical heat was so unbearable. Susan's noble efforts ended up being more like confinement in a slave-labor camp.

Before arriving in Balize, Susan was instructed that there would be "additional kitchen helpers" from the town people. But for some unknown reason, there were no helping hands. All meal preparation, serving and cleanup, was left to Susan. The medical team was gone for more than ten hours each day, giving shots and dispensing medicines to mothers with very sick children. When the team returned each evening, they were close to collapsing from heat exhaustion and usually passed up eating her elaborate meals. So, how could she dare complain or request help from any of them?

One night, most likely out of guilt, the team finally surrendered to the elegant dinner Susan had prepared for them. While proudly dishing up the plates, she noticed that her husband was missing from the company that politely endured her long, five-course meal. Naturally, she inquired of his whereabouts.

"Doc went up to bed about an hour ago," replied the beleaguered colleague with a sheepish smile. Most likely Don ducked out to avoid the guilt offering Susan was finally getting to serve his heroic medical team.

Susan might have been on the brink of divorce by the end of that mission trip. Her stint on the mission field probably remains a sore subject with them, so I am reluctant to bring up the topic for any additional details. I am relying on my memory. As I recall, Don was not amused, even though Susan attempted to be a good sport when relating the gory details to us during a dinner date.

But I do remember anxiously waiting for Susan's return. I couldn't wait to hear how the team enjoyed all of our delicious recipes. Unfortunately, this was another example of *puttin' on the dog and gettin' bit!*

# Peanut Butter & Chocolate Fixes

My dear hubby is a true peanut butter junkie. In fact, he hides his stash of JIF to dip into when no one is around. When the coast is clear, he licks heaping scoopfuls of peanut butter right off the spoon. I've never caught him in the act, but I have plenty of proof that he's a full-blown addict.

My husband is a 6'5'' former offensive tackle with the NFL. In his glory days with the Detroit Lions, he was a fierce, first-round draft pick from Ohio State University. In college, in the mid-sixties, under Coach Woody Hayes, Daryl helped lead his team to victory in a championship game against the University of Michigan. No grizzly football tackle would ever dream this hunk of a man dunks Windmill Cookies in his coffee like a little kid.

As a typical addict, Daryl will go several months without binging. I can take or leave peanut butter, so I seldom buy it. So, whenever I discover his newly purchased jar of JIF on the highest shelf, hidden behind taller canned goods, I know he's fallen off the wagon. Another telltale sign is recurrent peanut butter coated spoons left in the sink.

One evening my two dogs and I slept together on the couch through the six o'clock news. A wicked summer thunderstorm jolted us awake and off the couch during *Who Wants to be a Millionaire?* Panicked that the roof might be on fire from the lightning bolt, I darted through the house like a wildcat in search of missing cubs. Our terrified boxers were hot on my heels. We found Mr. No Pulse calmly sitting on the sun porch, near an open window, clicking on his laptop, oblivious to the severe bolts of thunder, which struck about every sixty-seconds or so.

"Well, I suppose that last bolt of lightning woke up all you girls, didn't it?" He chuckled. Being scared out of my wits by demon-powered thunder was not amusing.

Half asleep, I was crabby from low blood sugar. I needed a quick fix. The dogs trailed me to the kitchen. Still in a daze, I wondered why my husband seemed so jovial. Then the mystery was solved. A lone, 40-ounce jar of JIF stood in blatant display on the kitchen counter. The bright red lid lay right next to it. It astonished me because I hadn't seen a sign of peanut butter-possession for at least six-months.

At the sight of the jar, a small plate of soda crackers spread with creamy peanut butter seemed like the perfect pick-me-up. By the time I scrounged around for a box of saltines in the back of the cereal cupboard, I was salivating. With a butter knife, I dipped in the JIF, but the jar was completely empty! My heart sank. Undaunted, I hungrily scraped enough peanut butter off the sides and bottom. It took several minutes to work off a single teaspoon for a lone cracker.

I sat back down on the couch to enjoy my hard-earned treat, but Zoey and Petra got a whiff. As I started to nibble on the peanut butter cracker, two pleading pairs-of-eyes met my gaze. After another small nibble, I shared the remaining meager snack with my Boxer buddies. It's the first taste of peanut butter for the near grown pups and each seemed totally elated.

My husband has another addiction, too. It's chocolate. When we were first married, I used to hide bags of chocolate chips in the back of the freezer, beneath the frozen hamburger. There's nothing more aggravating than whipping up butter, eggs, brown and white sugars with flour, only to discover the bag of semi-sweet chocolate chips is missing from the pantry drawer. The disappearance of chocolate chips happened more than once before I wised up.

I am smiling now, recalling another time in our marriage when my jittery husband began pacing the floors in need of a fix.

"I wish there was some chocolate around," he lamented, mindlessly pulling open drawers, as if a candy bar would actually last long enough to be stuffed way into storage. I didn't give in right away. But his pitiful sighs soon wore me down.

"Well, all right...If you're really that desperate, I'll tell you where there's some chocolate-chips hid." His face lit up even though it felt like I had finally caved into my interrogators.

"There's a bag of chocolate-chips hidden in the back of the freezer, buried under some packages of meat," I reluctantly confessed, regretting the disclosure of such a clever hiding spot.

"Oh." His countenance fell. "I ate that bag a month ago."

# Best Ever Cookie Secret Revealed

A few decades ago, Daryl and I joined Dave and Anne for a 4th of July potluck at their house.

While the guys shot hoops in the driveway out back, our hostess spontaneously whipped up a warm batch of chocolate-chip cookies as a bonus treat. Side-by-side in her kitchen, we chatted as she stirred the ingredients of a single batch of cookie dough. I didn't pay much attention. But, when she dumped in two, 12-ounce bags of chocolate chips in the bowl for the single recipe, my eyes nearly popped out. I didn't say a word.

Later, as my husband bit into the gooey chocolate cookie, more chocolate than cookie, he smacked his lips. Holding up a half-eaten cookie for everyone to view, he declared, "Now these are the best chocolate-chip cookies I've ever eaten!" I felt like the runner-up in the 4-H Club bake-off competition. He'd always complain about my cookies.

Whenever I baked chocolate-chip cookies in the past, I would vary the recipe, trying to please him to no avail. It was the lone ratio of dough to double the amount chocolate chips that was the secret. Since being enlightened by Anne, I've swallowed my pride. She gets all the credit for the prize recipe and finally solving the baffling mystery of why my cookies were always considered a flop. I no longer scrimp on the chocolate chips when it comes to homemade cookies. At last, I found the secret to a happy husband. Instead of using only a single bag of chocolate chips for a *doubled-dough* recipe, I now double the chocolate-chips for a single dough recipe for my ever-happy chocolate-lover. Now I won't go to my grave wondering what went wrong in our marriage.

# Stashing for Sanity Sake

About forty-five-years ago, Marlo Thomas, the television star, married Phil Donahue, a popular daytime television host. It seemed like a match-made-in-heaven, except for Phil's rambunctious, teenage boys from a previous marriage.

In a magazine interview, the famous and glamorous stepmother explained that she could never keep enough groceries in the house because the fellows inhaled food. She confessed to "hiding Oreo cookies in my lingerie drawer so the boys wouldn't gobble them up." I could relate since I had two step-kids of my own.

One summer night, early in our marriage, my husband came to bed about 11 p.m. Having fallen asleep earlier, I awakened with severe cottonmouth. An ice-cold Coca-Cola was all I could think about as I hurried downstairs to the kitchen. Our stinky tap water, from a well, was full of sulfur, so I was probably dehydrated the entire two years we lived in Centerville, Ohio. Back in those days, buying "bottled" water seemed as extravagant as purchasing caviar for an everyday appetizer.

As a perpetual dieter, there are certain times in life when nothing satisfies like drinking an ice-cold bottle of Coke, calories in all. Not diet cola, pure Coke – the real thing. It was one of those rare moments for me.

Just two days before, I had stocked up on ten, 2-liter bottles of Coke and 7-Up for the kids. My stepchildren were about eleven and twelve at this time.

Half asleep, I trailed downstairs through the dark house to pour myself a small glass of Coke to satisfy my thirst. To my dismay, all ten refundable, glass bottles were bone dry. My step kids and their friends had guzzled down 680 ounces of pop in a forty-eight-hour period!

Disheartened, I had to settle for a diet soda. Even though the kids hated diet pop, my secret stash was hidden under the kitchen sink. The 8-pack of Diet Vernors had screw-on-bottle tops; therefore, weekly inventory was quickly taken by a quick peek for missing bottle caps. I reached down, groping under the sink for a bottle of Vernors. Relieved to see that all the dark bottle caps were on, I pulled up a bottle to drink. Oddly, it was empty. Thinking it was a manufacturer's glitch, I reached for another capped bottle. Empty again! I quickly jerked up six more empty bottles in disbelief. All the bottle caps were purposely screwed back on to appear as full bottles! Those little devils!

When I burst through the bedroom door, my husband was cozy under the covers reading a spy novel. He looked up with an inviting smile, which quickly changed to stunned disbelief. His eyes widened.

I was as distraught as if my pet dog had just been run over. I trembled from head to toe. Naturally, Daryl was extremely alarmed. In those first two-years of marriage, he had never seen me break down before that moment. He sprang up from his pillow in a flash. "What's wrong? What's the matter?' Tell me what's wrong with you!"

You know, in the journey of life, it's never a monumental event that pushes one over the edge. It's an accumulation of uneventful circumstances that fester beneath the surface, springing forth to strangle when you least expect it. Sometimes it takes years to reach that breaking point. Then, suddenly, out of the blue, some tiny, insignificant event triggers a deep seeded succession of unforgotten or unforgiven travesties that completely flip you out. It must be true that a straw can break a camel's back.

With a heaving chest, I clung to the wall for support. At that point of my meltdown, I grieved too hard to speak. I somehow managed to gasp out unintelligible sounds like an anguished woman who'd lost her only son in the war.

Finally, the truth came forth with a heaving chest, "They…(sob)…drank…(sob)…all…(sob)…the…(sob)…pop"

Without a word, Daryl leaped out of bed. He snatched his slacks off the chair and dashed through the door as if the house was in flames. A few moments later, I peeked out the bedroom window in time to witness his car roar from the garage. Peeling rubber out of the driveway, he sped off to the nearest 7-Eleven store faster than an ambulance driver. He returned twenty-minutes later with a six-pack of diet 7-UP as a peace offering, which I sheepishly accepted. We never discussed my meltdown. Apparently, he got the point, though. Besides, I didn't have the heart to tell him that I was actually craving a Coke.

# Cherished Senior Moments

The email arrived from my husband, Daryl, away on his weekly business trip. The subject line read, *"phone went thru wash."* His message said, *"until i get a new one today or tomorrow can"t call, email. D."* (That's exactly how it was written.)

Please tell me this didn't go out to all his clients, too! I thought shaking my head in disbelief.

Semi-retirement requires an adaptable, makeshift aptitude and attitude when attempting to sail through daily mishaps, mechanical breakdowns, memory deficit and the loss of technical support such as misplaced car keys, eyeglasses, channel changers, and cell phones.

For the first time in more than three decades of marriage, my husband started insisting to doing his own laundry. "I'll do my own laundry," he grumbled. "Whenever anyone else does my wash, I always end up with stuff missing." Apparently on the last wash cycle, he forgot to remove his cell phone from a pants pocket.

As I am writing this, my wobbly, bifocal-glasses recently lost their protective rubber nose pads. To keep the sharp medal from irritating my skin, I have cushioned the bridge of my nose with a padding made of a folded piece of paper towel. I haven't looked in the mirror to see how ridiculous I must look, so if the doorbell rings, I hope I won't forget to remove my glasses.

Before I became a senior citizen, I expressed genuine sympathy for retired couples shopping together. Invariably, as I passed by, I'd hear the helpful hubby challenge her mental capacities. "Now why are you buying this brand? This other label is so much cheaper." Pity would ooze from my eyes for the meek little woman who looked trapped.

About twenty-five years ago, my husband and I went on a rare grocery-shopping together. During that infamous trip, we bumped into a nice lady from our church. She held up a fistful of coupons and began rattling off all the money she saves while shopping.

At the far end of the aisle, Daryl politely remained attentive to the joys of couponing while I wandered off with my cart to continue shopping. As I placed the large jar of mayonnaise in the basket, his big booming voice roared, "We don't need any more mayonnaise. Put it back!" That was the last time we ventured into the grocery store together unless we made a pact not to refute each other's purchases. I refuse to be pitied by some thirty-year-old overhearing any dispute on my selection of a favorite brand name in my shopping cart.

When I buy gas, if my car is dirty, I opt for a discount car wash with each fill-up. However, one day, my husband came home and denounced that system. "That stupid car wash left a streak of soapsuds on my trunk lid. Now the finish is permanently damaged!"

Recently, after going through this same auto-wash, I pulled out into traffic. An elderly African-American man, riding in the passenger seat of a nearby vehicle, leaned out his window with a big, friendly smile. He began waving at me with both hands, dramatically pointing to the rear of my car. I grinned and waved back, assuming that it was soap suds left on my rear bumper of my candy-apple red Coupe Deville. However, when I got home, I discovered that the gas tank door was open and the gas cap was dangling down. I had driven through the car wash with my gas tank wide open!

# Missing Teeth & Missing Glasses

This past year, Daryl needed extensive dental work for two missing molars. The dentist advised him not to have implants since they had failed in years past. If Daryl smiled, the missing teeth were a noticeable gap. His partial dentures require special care, and he's finally getting used to them. However, the first few months he'd often forget to put them in his mouth. Often in social settings or in church, he would lean over and say, "Can you believe it? I forgot my teeth again."

One summer day my Aunt Katie fetched the mail, but she couldn't locate the reading glasses she'd been using moments before the mail arrived. She searched the house for hours. Finally, after re-tracking her steps outside she found them. She laughed, "The glasses were on the hood of my car where I placed them when I came out for the mail!"

I'd be rich if I got a nickel every time my husband said, "Have you seen my glasses?"

My friend Anne agreed. She gleefully replied, "Oh! That used to be me. I got so fed up searching for my reading glasses, that I purchased about twenty pair from a discount store. Now I never have to hunt to see."

# Lost & Found

Nothing's more aggravating than not being able to locate the remote channel changer when your favorite television program is about to start. One such time the "clicker" remained lost for several days. I finally called the cable company to have a new one shipped, which took another three days to arrive. I eventually found the old remote control clinging to inside my cosmetic storage case that opens like a toolbox.

One day I entered a shopping mall and quickly realized I'd left my cell phone in the car. But when I returned to the car, it was nowhere to be found. Returning to the store, I smiled at the sales clerk. "Excuse me, would you call my cell phone for me? It's lost somewhere in my car. Just wait three minutes to give me time to get back out to the parking lot." She gave me a knowing smile. It worked. When I returned to the car, I found it ringing under the dashboard, hidden under a single piece of paper.

It's amazing how intuitive women are when helping other desperate females search for things. One night I was making a last-minute purchase just as Macy's department store was closing. A well-dressed African-American woman rushed up to my sales clerk. She was frantic. "I was just in here, and I can't find my car keys anywhere! My keys were on the counter when I bought this dress." This indeed was a serious matter since the store was ready to close within seconds. The lady held a plastic garment bag tied shut at the bottom.

The clerk quickly checked all around the counter and on the floor, to no avail. Instinctively I said, "Untie your garment bag, maybe the keys are in there." Her face lit up. Women have common radar when it comes to missing articles, and we stick together until that something is found. I would have offered to drive the dear lady home if she had not found those car keys. Her face radiated with hope as she quickly untied the knotted plastic bag. The keys fell to the floor with a lovely clank. I felt like a hero. It was the happiest sound I'd heard all year!

# The Bad Breath "Bible"

While driving my car, I once heard an advertisement for the *Bad Breath Bible*. I thought I was hearing things. Claiming to be the cure-all answer for halitosis, the handbook features everything to know about bad breath and how to cure it. Since this *Bad Breath Bible* is a limited edition, listeners were encouraged to order quickly. I heard this ad while listening to Fox News on my XM satellite radio. A Viagra advertisement immediately followed this one on bad breath.

One hundred years from now, when historians analyze our radio and television advertisements about Viagra and hair replacement, they'll be convinced that our men were all bald, impotent, and had bad breath. Those frequent ads for fresher breath and bath and body products will reveal our terror of having bad breath or body odor.

There's actually a *Smell Well* with Dr. Mel on the World Wide Web. He's a microbiologist whose Bad Breath web site answers most questions on the subject. Dr. Mel features an extensive list of related topics to click on; so, out of curiosity, I did some clicking on his site.

Dr. Mel invites feedback on bad breath problems. A huge challenge for him to address is "how to delicately tell people if they have bad breath." I'm very tempted to email Dr. Mel and share the approach my husband tried on me without having to say, "You have smelly breath."

One Sunday in church my husband offered me a mint. I said, "No, thanks." In a solemn tone, he replied, "Yes, you really do want one." I was mortified.

For millions who are afflicted with diabetes and suffer with acetone breath, I'm not making light of this unfortunate condition. However, the American Diabetes Association should make known that bad breath is a side of effect of this disease. Preventing blindness, stroke and early death doesn't seem to motivate people to get tested, but the fear of getting bad breath might!

Body odor is in a class of its own. Europeans claim that Americans are obsessed with smelling good. They're probably right.

A few years ago I was embarking on a goodwill trip to Odessa, Ukraine, with a group of mission-minded churchwomen. Along with medicine, clothing, and medical equipment, we were taking ourselves as goodwill ambassadors from our local church.

We boarded the jumbo jet and settled in our cramped, coach seats for the lengthy trip. Our seat assignments were located in a side section with two seats per row. My husband looked important, so he was upgraded to business class. I didn't mind because his legs are much longer than mine. The rest of our female team was in pairs, seated in the three rows in front of me. When no one showed for the vacated seat next to me, it looked as if I would get to spread out for the long haul across the Atlantic Ocean. In fact, my girlfriends were teasing that I probably "pulled a fast one with the booking agent."

However, to my dismay, right before take-off, an old woman, hunched over, donning a dingy babushka, appeared struggling in the aisle. Laden with huge, overstuffed bags, she was assisted by the flight attendant. My heart sank when she looked in my direction to locate the woman's seat. My hopes of having that extra seat to myself were quickly dashed.

Sure enough, my 10-hour seatmate plopped down, smiling, nodding, and speaking in Russian, radiant to return to her motherland. She also reeked of body odor. It was unbearable. After the seatbelt signal went off, the church ladies took pity on me. They volunteered to do "missionary duty" by taking turns sitting next to her. However, they could only tolerate fifteen-minute shifts, unless we hit turbulence and had to stay belted in our seats.

This dear Russian lady couldn't speak a word of English, but she communicated well with her cherub face and expressive blue eyes. She had no idea that we considered her body odor offensive. We managed to smile, nod, clap, and treat her with respect, but it took every bit of Jesus inside us to do so.

As it turned out this woman was a prophetic "sign" of what was ahead once we arrived in Odessa. As a throw-back to Communism, the city officials still controlled the hot water and the heat throughout the entire city. In the summer months, for most parts of the city, there was no hot water available. Hot water was turned on sometime in November and shut off in May; ditto for the heat. During the winter months the heat was randomly shut off in certain sectors of the city for no reason at all. The privileged purchased their own water heaters, if they could find them on the black market.

We arrived in late March to a blizzard. To keep warm, we wore three and four layers of clothing to bed. I also slept under a small, heavy floor rug for added protection from the bitter cold. The hotel did offer some hot water, but only during certain times of the day or night. If gone from the room during the "warm-water visitation," we missed out. In the frigid morning, it was too cold to shower or to change clothing. B.O was the least of our worries. Thermal long johns suddenly took on a new meaning. Survival took precedent over blow dryers, curling irons, and mascara.

When our team returned home, we all had B.O, bad breath, and bags under our eyes. But no one seemed to mind, considering it was only a temporary hardship. How grateful we were to return to our hot showers and warm beds!

It seems that our American obsession with B.O and bad breath can be cured on the mission field.

# Pop the Clutch... Huh?

"**N**o cruise control? Are you *serious?* How can we get a car without cruise control! Driving all the way to Florida, with no cruise! Dude, we're going to get hit with so many tickets!"

Today, at Meijer, a Midwest mega-mart grocery chain, I heard those strong exclamations while standing at the customer service counter, returning two, wrong-size, leather belts. The nearby customer, a twenty-something young man, was blurting out his frightening car news to a same-age, same-sex friend, who worked behind the lottery-ticket counter.

After my refund, I rushed past the two young men to hear the lottery-ticket clerk exclaim, "Oh, my God, for an entire decade my mom...." I missed the rest of the crisis, but "not having cruise control," certainly stirred my thoughts.

At their age the first car I drove had a stick shift, no air conditioning, hand-crank windows, and, worst of all, no automatic door locks. Driving friends around without auto locks became a nuisance because the driver had to stretch all the way across the bench-seat and unlock the passenger door. And in those days, three girls drove in the front seat while original Beatles music blared, with new songs arriving each week.

After leaving the store with my nostalgia stirred, I regretted not sticking around to hear the tail end of that interesting saga. So, out of curiosity, after getting into my car, I called the store from my cell phone and requested the lottery-ticket counter. "James" answered the phone.

"Hi, James. I was at the service counter a minute ago, and I overheard your conversation about cars. I am very curious to find out what your mother has been doing for 'an entire decade.'"

"Oh, yeah," he responded with a chuckle. "My mom gets so many speeding tickets that she's almost lost her license. She lives in California and drives to work on some real long, straight roads. She gets to her limit of tickets, waits three years to get one dropped, then she gets another speeding ticket."

"Oh, I know what you mean," I replied, continuing the conversation, as if we were old comrades. "In Colorado, the speed limit is 75 miles an hour, so you know everyone drives faster than that. My stepdaughter lives out there. Last year, she got so many tickets that they made her attend those weekend classes with all the DUI's, and she doesn't even drink!"

That night at the dinner table with my husband and our adult son, Bo, I related my conversation with James.

Bo has an older sister and brother from my husband's teen marriage. I explained to Bo that his sister usually drives in the fast lane, and in Colorado, that's at least 80 mph. If she is distracted by her cell phone or conversation with someone in car, she slows down a bit. But, if the car behind her attempts to pass on the right, she gets mad and punches down on the gas pedal and yells, "Oh, no, you don't!" So far, no one has ever successfully accomplished passing her because she guns it and shoots ahead like a character in the movie *Fast and the Furious*.

My husband chimed in, looking at Bo. "Oh, yeah, she's worse than her brother when it comes to getting mad at other drivers. That's iniquity passed down through the bloodline. And it comes from Herb. My dad was just like that when he used to drive."

Bo quipped, "Herb really must have been notorious. He's always getting blamed for all the family flaws."

We burst out laughing.

Actually, my dear father-in-law was a happy, fun loving guy. But being from that particular generation, Herb left a hefty pile of excess baggage for his kids to examine from time-to-time.

For instance, Herb detested anyone chomping down food or making crunching noises while eating. God forbid if anyone ate celery or crunched on peanuts within earshot of him. Unfortunately, all the Sanders men possess this same "iniquity," as my husband affectionately refers to this idiosyncrasy passed down through the genes. Sometimes we just call these annoyances, "Herb-isms."

One Sander's male made his wife to leave the room whenever she munched on a crunchy apple.

After 40 plus years of marriage, I still don't chew gum in front of my husband because it's no fun chewing a wad of gum without cracking it to death.

One time a new employee during a luncheon meeting nervously crunched an entire cup of ice throughout the long, extended staff meeting. I thought Daryl was going to have a coronary, but the boss suffered through like a prisoner of war.

Years ago, I helped Lorraine, my sister-in-law, hang flowered wallpaper in her dining room in time for the family Easter brunch the next day. Under extreme pressure to finish, we were both cracking our chewing gum like clucking hens in a crowded chicken coop. Stepping back to admire our work, I casually remarked, "Boy, it's a good thing Daryl's isn't here. He's be going out of his mind listening to our jaws cracking gum!"

Lorraine looked at me. "Oh, your brother is the same way. Dave glares at me if he's within twenty feet of me chewing. So, trust me, I've been in my total glory being able to snap in peace!" I sure hope my brother doesn't pass that idiosyncrasy down to his son.

At dinner tonight after we finally stopped chuckling about Herb getting blamed again, my husband said, "Yeah, in high school, when I went out on a date, I used to have to park his old '53 Studebaker on a hill, so I could roll down the hill to pop the clutch."

Bo looked bewildered. "Pop the clutch?"

This is a generation gypped out of growing up with cars without door-locks, cruise-control, central air and, worst of all, never knowing the joys of having high school friends push your old man's Chevy down a hill, just to get it running again.

How did we ever survive such hardships?

# Sideline Peep Show

My former bum left shoulder once placed me in a 92-degree, water-therapy pool at a medical health center several times a week. My physician warned that my lame, left limb will stiffen up to a dreaded "frozen shoulder" if I didn't keep at it. The heated pool was wonderful. By listening to chatty, arthritic seniors soaking up the heat, I stayed abreast on new restaurants, die-hard eating places, dining spots to avoid, good flicks to see and bad ones to boycott, high cost insurance rates, and current retirement benefits. I also heard charming grandchild exploits.

As a former synchronized swimmer in junior high, I love the water, even though I am out of shape and out of breath most of the time. I manage to stretch and pull those rigid muscles, which seems to help, because my shoulder is on the mend.

Mindy is a slender and spunky physical therapist that was a comic relief while enduring those painful water sessions. One afternoon she began telling me fascinating things about being on staff at this center. One night she turned on the water valves to replenish the diminished pool water to the proper level. But she forgot to shut off the water before going home for the night.

"The next morning, water had flooded all the way out to the dining area. But, I redeemed myself a few days later, when I smelled smoke from a overheated gas dryer in the laundry room."

Then Mindy spiced things up a bit. One afternoon she entered the pool area with a middle-age gentleman, her therapy patient. A young, shapely woman was perched on the poolside deck, wearing a skimpy bikini. She was doing some exotic yoga stretches on her back. Suddenly the lady's lanky legs were wrapped around her neck and she seemed oblivious to all the old men gawking at her inverted Lotus-positioned crotch. Mindy mimicked her patient's reaction, lowering her voice to sound gruff like him.

"Now where was she when I was single!" declared the guy, ogling in complete astonishment.

# Crazy College Antics!

One morning Mindy entered the warm, therapy pool with a pudgy, twenty-something guy named Mark who was obviously mentally challenged. The young man and his therapist promptly placed long, blue noodles under their armpits to stay afloat near me in the deep end. We were the only three bodies lavishing in the warmth of the pool.

She began telling us about her former job in the cafeteria while attending college.

Since Mark's job is delivering food trays to patients at the nearby hospital, Mindy asked to hear about "any occupational hazards" on his job. He thought for a few minutes. "Well, patients always complain and they act like it's my fault when they get rotten food."

"Oh, you see all kinds of weirdo things working in commercial kitchens," declared Mindy, picking up the slack. "When I worked in a college cafeteria, every 'Hamburger Tuesday,' the football team stuffed tons of burgers in their gym bags to eat later. They were allowed to consume all they wanted in the dining hall, but they couldn't take any food out with them."

Mark, being a mentally challenged young man, didn't seem to get it. But he volunteered his own childhood story. One Saturday morning his older sister was supposed to get up early and make the little guy breakfast. She refused to budge, so he dumped cold water on her to get even. We laughed with him because he was so tickled remembering that event. Up to that point he seemed puzzled hearing all of Mindy's silly anecdotes.

Hearing this prank reminded her of the antics she pulled off in college. "Rhonda from Lincoln County, West Virginia" was Mindy's notorious roommate in the dorm. Rhonda egged Mindy on to do insane things, which frequently got them both in trouble. "Rhaah on- da" had such a thick, Ohio Valley drawl that Mindy quickly picked up her accent. She imitated Rhonda with an exaggerated twang. Mindy's mother refused to let her call home until she stopped sounding like some hillbilly from Appalachia.

"One-time," she continued with a chuckle, "Rhonda and I put about a cup of baby powder in a long envelope and carefully cut open both ends. Then we rigged up a blow dryer, inserting the nozzle inside through an open end. We slipped the other open end under the dormitory door of some snobbish girl we couldn't stand. We turned on the blow dryer, which blew the white powder all over the place. Everything she touched would be covered with volcano-like ash. Afterwards we greased the doorknob with Vaseline, so all the dust would get stuck to her hands."

Mindy was on a roll after hearing me laugh so hard.

"But the most trouble Rhonda and I got into was for our fake striptease show for the boy's dormitory across from ours. We often caught those little perverts peeking in our windows, so we decided to put on a real show for them. I put on a bikini to appear naked and piled on about four layers of clothing to take off slowly. Rhonda put on a dance CD to get us in the mood. She pointed a floodlight at the window shade, so all the guys could see was my silhouette. I stood on a table and began slowly pealing off pieces of clothing like a real stripper." It was reported to security and to the President of the University that "two girls were putting on a girly show for the boys." So when the two culprits showed up in the R.A.'s office for discipline, she cried out, "Oh no! Not you two again! I can't even deal with this now – get out of here!"

Now it was my turn to chime in. "Oh, I had a friend just like Rhonda in college. She was a girl from New Jersey named Pam."

In September, 1965, Carol, my dear friend from childhood, and I arrived at Northern Michigan University in our preppy Weejun penny loafers, stitched down pleated shirts with coordinated Garland ribbon sweaters and very calm hair. We were anxious to meet our two new suitemates. A common bathroom, shared by all four girls, connected two dorm rooms.

I first spotted Jersey Girl in her room, which adjoined ours through the bathroom. I hurried back to warn Carol that a gang member from "West Side Story" shared our bathroom. If the movie "Grease" had been out yet Pam could have played the character Rizzo perfectly. At first Pam scared us, but she quickly grew on us. Pam's boorish roommate promptly moved out, finding a different room to occupy. So, it was just the three of us, making it tempting to stay up late in Pam's room and laugh until we were breathless.

Pam had lacquer coated, black hair, ratted a mile high. She used empty, concentrated orange-juice cans to roll her naturally curly hair up each night. On the wall, opposite our bathroom mirror, was a shiny ring of lacquer from all the heavy doses of hair spray that Pam used continuously throughout the day and night to keep her hair from kinking. Pam had pale skin and wore heavy, black eye make-up, outlining her eyes with thick Maybelline eyebrow pencil. Pam was tall and gangly. She wore skin-tight straight skirts and matching sweaters over her well-padded bra. Pam was so self-conscious about her flat chest that her actual breast size remained an American unsolved mystery. If Pam changed her bra in front of us, she placed the clean one over the one she'd been wearing and carefully slipped the previous bra off without showing an inch of skin. In fact, she wore a padded bra under her pajamas each night.

Pam was feisty and ornery at times, resenting her wealthy parents, who bribed her to attend college instead of cosmetology school. The first few weeks of school she cried a lot while wailing tears of lament for being so far from home. Pam habitually slept through all her early core-classes and soon flunked out, so in the end, she got back at them.

Pam was also a goofball character like Lucille Ball, in "I Love Lucy" because she had the same zany personality. Pam didn't like Anne Marie, our goody-two shoe dorm R.A, who ran the second floor. Pam could mimic Anne Marie's squeaky voice and the way her eyes rolled up in the sockets whenever our R.A had to address broken house rules with us, which was quite often.

The first time Anne Marie came to room 213 to speak to all of us, Pam peered upward, wondering what she was looking at. We all figured it out. But every time Anne Marie spoke to us with pupils pointing north, Pam mockingly searched the ceiling just to make Carol and me have to stifle the urge to burst out laughing.

One night during a snowstorm, Pam felt ornery and decided to play a prank on all the hard-working academic students she resented, and Anne Marie. We occupied room 213, so Pam began telephoning every girl from room 212 on down to room 200. It was 3 am, and I was the partner in this devilish scheme.

"Hello, this is Anne Marie. There's going to be a fire drill in 5 or 10 minutes, so wake-up your roommate and get prepared to go outside," warned Pam, in a hushed, whiny voice.

Soon twelve, descending toilets began flushing one after the other, as the twenty-four or more academe came out of a coma-like sleep to face the "fire drill." We imagined the girls bumping in to each other, groping around for warm clothes, and ripping out hair rollers, since most of us religiously rolled our hair in curlers every night. God forbid we'd allow any boys to see us in curlers at 3:10 a.m.! Obviously, blow dryers, curling irons and hot rollers had not reached the general public yet.

Pam and I took a quick peek down the hall. About eight girls were lined up against the wall, in heavy coats, looking very sleepy, waiting for the fire drill to go off.

Someone banged on our door, so we had to act as if we had just awakened.

A girl burst through the room as Pam began rubbing her eyes and yawning. "Hey, what the heck is going on out there? Who's making all that noise?"

"If your phone rings, let me answer it!" shouted the angry student. "It's someone pretending to be Anne Marie, telling us there's going to be a fire drill!"

Carol slept through the whole drama and went on to graduate from college.

The next day, Pam was loading a washing machine, with her usual Marlboro cigarette dangling from her lips. A hapless victim of the prank wandered in the second-floor laundry room, yawning, and complaining of extreme fatigue. The weary fellow student had been wide-awake since 3 am and explained why. With huge, bug-eyes, Pam said, "Now who'd ever play such a dirty, rotten trick on someone? That is just awful! Whoever did that, deserves to get kicked out of school!" Pam's halo stayed in tack and so did mine.

# Memory Lapses Last
# Longer Than Diets

After 4½ days, my dieting plans perished with pizza. Last Saturday was to blame. The death spiral of my short-lived discipline began when I joined two friends for coffee at Cracker Barrel. While chatting with my longtime friend, Bonnie, and a thirty-something Marianna, I mindlessly began digging around in my large, canvas bag, a Mother's Day gift from my husband Daryl and son Bo. All the while I was rummaging, I kept on yakking. After a frustrating few minutes, I looked up, confused. "What am I looking for!" I was beleaguered because it was another familiar "Senior Moment." Allison, my thirty-something niece always mutters, "Old!" to her parents, anytime Fred or Florence pause to fetch a word. But, it's really no laughing matter.

However, Bonnie, closer to my postmenopausal era, completely sympathized.

She quipped, "Oh, Bob and I spend more time these days looking for things we can't find around the house. It drives us nuts!"

With that, Bonnie and I started howling. We couldn't stop laughing for several minutes. After gasping for breath, Bonnie choked out, "Ginkgo Biloba, double-strength, really helps me a lot!" Thirty-year-old Marianna stared at us with a blank expression on her face.

Whatever I was looking for in that deep designer bag must not have been that important, I concluded, parking it back on the seat next to me. It wasn't worth fretting about. That's the trouble with those oversized totes – they keep filling up with so much stuff that you can't find anything in them.

Later, we drove to Bonnie's nearby house for additional fellowship. It was a warm early summer evening. While standing out on Bonnie's driveway, we reminisced about our childhood while munching down frozen chocolate treats from an old-fashioned, family owned ice cream truck. Marianna drives it during her summer-leave from nursing. There's good money in it, and it's far more fun rounding up children with that excitable, well-known ringing bell.

When I arrived home that same evening, I was starving. Since I considered that my diet was officially blown by ice cream consumption, I ordered a small pizza from a local place that delivers. After all, if you're going to cheat on a diet, make it worthwhile!

As I was brushing my teeth the next morning before church, I looked in the mirror. To my dismay, a puffy lump had appeared under my left eye, about half the size of a pepperoni. I was horrified. At my age, I never banked on getting bags under my eyes from water retention and too much sodium by eating pepperoni pizza.

After a recent bone density test, my same-age-same-sex doctor wrote me a note across the bottom of my report. "Must be nice to have the bones of a thirty-year-old!" Dr. Tallo was probably envious; but, then again, she's a toothpick. It's usually a trade-off. Ever notice? Someone wearing Coke-bottle lens glasses usually has perfect teeth. An acne-prone woman with bad skin usually is tiny and petite. Crooked or buckteeth – thick eye lashes. Thunder thighs, pretty face. There is really no such thing as an ideal body with a pretty face, except in Hollywood. So much for all that cheese and ice cream I've eaten in life – the one consolation is that I'm consuming calcium for my solid bones.

Come to think of it, another beneficial thing about my body weight is that I breezed through menopause during the last few years. I have yet to experience a single hot flash. Knock on wood. A true miracle, that is, if I don't count my memory lapses as the trade-off.

# Squirt Bottle Cure All

Whenever I return home, my loveable female Boxers, Petra and Zoey, twirl at full speed, dipping and diving, as though I've been missing for a month.

However, my more serious concern is their aggressive, territorial feuds over chewable bones or who's stationed on my lap late at night.

"Mom, you need a water bottle," Elisa quipped. "I squirt Kit whenever he jumps up on our computer. Now that darn cat stops dead in his tracks if he just spots that bottle!" The oldest of my adult twin daughters, spoke with the authority of a prison warden.

Early the next day I gleefully filled my six, newly purchased Dollar Store squirt bottles and placed them in strategic spots throughout the family room. All bright yellow nozzles were set at the strongest, fastest speed for perfect aim. I confess I was eager to try it out. I didn't have to wait long. When the dogs started to gnarl at each other in a playful, but aggressive manner, I commanded, "Stop!" They completely ignored me. When I shot Petra in the face, her stunned reaction made me start to laugh, but I didn't dare let out the happy howl I suppressed.

Yesterday, over a lone bone, they went at it like demon-possessed pit bulls during a prizefight. Just two strong water squirts stopped the brawl. It was pure magic!

When my younger brother was a toddler, he'd hold his breath during a temper tantrum. He'd turn cobalt blue. One very hot summer in 1950, while we vacation traveled through the Smokey Mountains, his face turned purplish-black in the back seat. In sheer panic, Mom grabbed a bottle of cold milk out of the ice cooler and dumped it over his head. That did it. He gasped in shock and started to breathe. I strongly suspect my exasperated mother continued to splash his face with each reoccurring tantrum.

Too bad we can't use it on annoying, obnoxious people.

"Okay, I can take the next in line," announces the newly arrived cashier, nonchalantly glancing in your direction and the four or five people lingering behind you. You've been standing in line for 9 minutes and are running late for an appointment.

The reprobate directly behind you ducks out of line, darting toward the alternate check out counter, refusing to look back in your direction. Imagine having a squirt bottle in your purse.

"I was the next in line!" Take aim. Squeeze! First squirting the mindless cashier, then a double squirt at the moron who took your rightful place at the checkout counter.

Or how about a grouchy husband or the belligerent teenager?

"Okay," Hubby grumbles, "what'd you do with TV remote?"

Squirt!

You'd have to invest in many more squirt bottles to keep them on hand. They'd surely cure all sorts of community grievances and pet peeves!

# Scandalously Clad
# Costume Party

My friend Susan is a gourmet cook, now infamous for her cherry strudel and extravagant dinner parties. About thirty years ago she got the brainstorm to have a costume party in honor of Bea's birthday.

In her former and forsaken life, our friend, Bea, had been a famous Rockette at New York City's Radio City Music Hall. Purely for the shock value, Susan, the informant, loved to reveal this juicy tidbit of information because I only knew Bea as an ultraconservative, serious scholar, close to obtaining her doctorate at Ohio State University. For Bea's birthday party, the guest of honor was going to arrive dressed as a bumblebee, in a clever handmade black and yellow striped costume, complete with wings. Susan planned to wear all black, paint a white mask on her face like a mime and wear a pointed clown's hat. Don would rent a Civil War uniform. The other invited guests were not allowed entrance unless they were dressed in a costume.

Daryl and I had just been to Chicago for the International Dance Festival. I managed to drag my husband to all six performances, so I could lovingly gaze at Mikhail Baryshnikov, at the peak of his outstanding dance career.

"Hey, Daryl and I could come as famous dancers. We can dress him in leotards and he could come as Mikhail Baryshnikov and I'd be Margot Fontaine." I was only kidding.

Susan's face lit up with mischievous delight. "If you can talk him into doing that I will be forever indebted to you!" she cried in glee, begging me to follow through with the flamboyant notion.

Amazingly, Daryl agreed to don tights for the costume party. Making sure I wouldn't chicken out, Susan escorted me downtown to a dance-attire store to purchase the male ballet tights and to make serious inquiries about the under garments. After all, we didn't want my husband hanging out at the party.

"What do they wear under their ... well, you know...is there a special jock strap?" I asked, feeling my cheeks flush.

Susan and I giggled like silly schoolgirls. The effeminate sales clerk was not at all amused, as he seriously explained the options of every male dancer while performing in tights.

My conservative husband, the former NFL offensive tackle, was talked into this crazy scheme. I think he did it just for Susan, knowing how delighted she would be to see him in drag.

At the time of the party, we were physically fit enough to pull off some smooth dance movements for the shrieking party crowd. Our Pas de Deux was a fitting tribute to Dr. Bea Edelstein, the former Rockette.

# The Stork's Surprise Visit

On a Monday, a few months after the scandalous costume party, Bea and I arrived to help Susan prepare complicated appetizers for Bea's college graduation party on Friday. However, the famous party giver had cut it too close to the due date of her highly anticipated baby adoption.

Working with Phyllo dough can be tricky business because it's as thin as tissue paper. It quickly dries out and flakes, so the layers must be kept under damp dishtowels. The best of chef's have difficulty handling it. The Greek recipe was individual, one-inch squares of Phyllo dough, painted with melted butter, using a pastry brush, repeating the process three more times. Next, the buttered layers were topped with a dab of a cheese concoction, before quickly folding it in a perfect triangle to resemble a folded up American Flag. Susan could freeze them in advance. On the day of the party, she could pull them straight from the freezer to bake, turning out hot crispy golden-brown delicacies to hungry guests.

Everything was going along smoothly until she discovered that Dr. Bea was not able to maneuver the dough properly. Like a military drill sergeant, Susan, hovered over us – moving back and forth from one table end to the other, inspecting every fold that our fingers managed. And she was not in the least bit diplomatic about correcting Bea's inept ability to fill and fold to perfection properly.

"I just can't get this technique -- I am all thumbs," said Bea with exasperated resolution. Not missing her opportunity, Bea was banished to kitchen-cleanup by the commander-in-chief of the kitchen. There is no beating around the bush by Susan when it comes to cooking. After Bea was out of earshot, Susan looked at me and shook her head. "How can anyone that smart not catch on to something so simple?" I just smiled. Bea was in agony the entire time that she was attempting to master something as complicated as Phyllo dough. For Bea, the kitchen cleanup had to be a welcome relief from the peer pressure of dough-duty.

But in all fairness, that morning, Susan received a thrilling, but terrifying phone call that Bethany was born! As an inexperienced mom, the expectant-adoptive-mother to be was entitled to be a little edgy in the midst of the Phyllo-dough-demonstration.

In addition to preparing for Bea's grand graduation party that Friday, Susan had Bea's parents as houseguests. Susan had no baby furniture because the attorney advised them "not to purchase anything until the papers were signed." After the appetizers were finished, we zoomed off to buy baby furniture. While in the store, Susan reminded me "to stay focused" because I was off trying to purchase bags of play sand for my son's sandbox. But, on Wednesday, when newborn baby Bethany arrived, I was focused with my movie-camera to capture another special moment with dear friends.

# Passages o Life

After asking a nearby shopper to lift a lone purple vase off the top shelf to place in my basket, I continued to mosey around housewares in the discount store. "Thank you, Sir." He smiled, but his wife gave me the evil eye.

As I turned the corner, our mini carts nearly collided in a kitchen aisle near an end cap containing stainless steel gadgets. The tall glamorous redhead looked like a movie star and slightly out of character in the discount department store. Rodeo Drive in Beverly Hills might be more appropriate for my dazzling friend who was golden brown from the sun, looking fabulous in an all-white cotton jacket. Susan's polished nails were long and perfect. Nearly every finger was enhanced with her signature diamond rings – the only woman I know who might wear that many glistening baubles for breakfast each morning.

"Well, hello! What are you doing at my end of town?" I asked, grinning from ear-to-ear. Susan and Don were our dearest friends, but it had been more than a year since we'd seen each other, although we talked frequently by phone.

After hugging, Susan easily produced a painter's stir stick from her designer purse. It was tinted a soft lavender.

"I drove all the over here to Burlington's trying to find a quilt to match this exact color for Abigail's new bed, but the store was closed down!"

"Oh, I know where their new location is. I just happened to

see it yesterday. Oh, look at these huge garlic presses! Have you seen any like these?"

"Yes. And they really work great," Susan said, taking the press from my hands. "Look, see how this extra piece slides back and forth? The outer skin doesn't get stuck like the other presses. I'm buying two – one for our condo in Florida and another for a shower gift."

"Then I'll get one, too." I said. You can always count on Susan to be up on the latest of everything.

We continued discussing the baby's bedroom, picking up pace, as we headed toward the linen section of the store. Even though we had not seen each other for more than a year, there was no need for the usual well, how have you been? Or the awkward what's new? Time diminishes between old friends; therefore, we didn't miss a beat. No further explanations were necessary. It was if we had traveling as a team all along, determined to find her soon-to-be-two, adorable granddaughter the perfect bedspread for her exalted departure from the crib.

"How's this one?" I asked, holding up a crib quilt in similar shades of purple and pink. I was thrilled to be part of the quest because watching Bethany grow up was very special to me. "Aunt" Barbara had been running the video when the adoption attorney handed five-day old baby Bethany into the anxious waiting arms of her new mother and father.

"That's nice, except it's a crib coverlet. I need something slightly larger, but smaller than a day bed, and they're awfully hard to find."

Like determined birddogs on the trail of a pheasant, we drove on to the new Burlington store before finding the perfect lavender sheet and blanket set at Baby's R Us three hours later. Afterward, we caught up with each other's lives during a leisurely two-hour dinner.

Susan gave me a blow-by-blow account of the day on their Florida beach when her son, Josh, got engaged to Lena. I hung on every detail because I had known her children since birth.

To pop the question in a surprise to Lena, Josh requested 12 dozen white roses under a rented, white tent set up on Siesta Key beach. Susan jumped into action and found 144 perfect white roses at a tremendous discount. She and her decorator friend pulled no stops with all the perfect pieces to go inside the tent. They covered a table and two chairs in white, creating a romantic setting perfect for the prince and princess. Don was dressed in a tuxedo ready to pour the champagne into stemmed glasses. " Not plastic ones, Mom. I want to hear the ting," Josh instructed.

Susan and her crew of girlfriends were hiding in the bushes peeking out as the couple strolled up from the beach. As Josh and Lena walked down the beach to view the sunset, a crowd had gathered off in the distance waiting for the thrilling surprise to unfold. Many of the single women watching were swooning over the grand gesture by this handsome romantic.

"Oh, what's this?" Josh asked, as he steered Lena toward the extravagant setting. When they entered the tent, Lena cried when she saw her future father-in-law in a tuxedo, smiling brightly. She realized that the countless white roses and glowing candles were for her – a treasured moment to remember forever. Josh seated her. On bent knee, Josh presented his love with a diamond ring. The hovering beach crowd had moved in for a closer peek. They cheered when Lena said "yes."

The story brought tears to my eyes. A photographer captured the moment, and the Sarasota News broke the story, along with the photograph, which ran that weekend.

After our wonderful day together, Susan called a week later to invite Daryl and me to a private family gathering to celebrate Abby's second birthday. The last time I had seen Bethany's baby was at Don's mother's funeral nearly a year ago, some months before that, we celebrated her 95th birthday party.

It's been wonderful to have dear friends to experience so many passages of life together.

# Surprises & Prizes

We arrived early, per Susan's request. "Please bring your camera and take some pictures of the baby before everyone gets here."

Dressed in bib overall shorts and barefoot, Susan was outside dashing across the front lawn to the house next door. "Park over there!" She hollered, waving, smiling madly, and pointing to her neighbor's driveway. Even in bibs, she still looked glamorous.

As soon as Daryl and I stepped out of the car, Susan quickly guided us by the elbows through the neighbor's garage door, leading into the kitchen.

"Just take a whiff of that!" she said, beaming. The aroma of Italian chicken cooking in her neighbor's spare oven was intoxicating. We followed her to the stove. Opening the oven door, Susan proudly displayed four huge pans of baked chicken. A gesture so like Susan – getting tickled over a sneak preview of the delicious feast that had probably taken two whole days to prepare.

When we arrived back at Susan's house, the darling two-year-old birthday girl was in a princess dress with a red Binkie pressed to her lips.

"Oh, my goodness! I was there when your mom bought this beautiful dress! She looks so adorable in it!" I exclaimed to Bethany.

Bethany's handsome husband, Josh, was holding the baby, who looked very much like Bethany at that same age. He was beaming as a proud Papa.

In front of the fireplace, the tiny bed was the focal point, complete with the lavender bedding that Susan and I had sought like a hidden treasure. She had taken a weathered, brown wooden-spindled child's bed and transformed it with a coat of crème colored paint. The details were accented in an array of pastels – pink, lavender, green, and yellow. It was perfect. Bright, colorful batches of Helium balloons were attached to the headboard. The elaborate array of colorfully wrapped birthday gifts was gracefully displayed on the gorgeous lavender blanket. Stretched across the mantel were about twelve festive gift bags for all the cousins who would arrive later.

Two-year old Abigail kept saying she wanted to open her "prizes" (surprises) and began pulling tissue from one of her bright gift bags. The bed was a complete surprise to Bethany, who was thrilled by her mother's ability to transform something so plain into a true work of art.

The manicured back yard featured Don's newly updated rock waterfall and fishpond. I chuckled when I spotted a freestanding sign that boldly read, "Thou Shalt Not Throw Rocks." On our unplanned Saturday outing, searching for the baby's bed quilting, Susan and I encountered a country craft store. We entered, hoping to find some homemade baby quilts in the right colors. Susan spotted the sign, which read something like Welcome to my garden. She bought it to repaint it, explaining why. Bailey, their other grandchild, is an adorable, but the rambunctious, nine-year old who had a blast throwing rocks in the water pond on her last visit. Unfortunately, the water lining was punctured. But the replacement ended up being an elaborate update and a much more exotic water pond.

When we were shopping together earlier that month, Susan had two princess dresses draped from her basket when I returned from the rest room.

"Which one do you like better?" It was hard to decide – they were both fabulous. "Well, since I need two different sizes, I'll get one of each."

"Is the other one for our Bailey girl?"

"Are you kidding? Bailey would never wear a dress like this. I would love it if she would. This other one is for the little girl next door."

Heidi, Don's beautiful and petite daughter from his first marriage, recently joined a professional women's football team, playing half back. Last week, Bailey's mother scored her first touchdown to a cheering crowd of proud parents and friends. Don chucked when he said Heidi's friends started chanting "Rudy, Rudy" after the Notre Dame movie of the same name. I thought they were pulling my leg until I saw pictures of Heidi in an actual football uniform, number 81, complete with a helmet and shoulder pads. Sunday was certainly full of surprises.

# Don't Get Caught in the Act!

Susan's dad was in the advance stages of Alzheimer disease. At her daughter, Bethany's baby shower, two years earlier, Susan's sister, Kathy, and her two sisters-in-law's were seated with me while we ate lunch in the dining room. They began explaining Dad's recent admission to a nursing home and the adventures that soon developed after he arrived. Their dad began asking to "go home," expressing a renewed interest in romance with their mother, who hasn't received that much attention from him in over two decades! Feeling sorry for her dad, Kathy coaxed, "Mom, when he gets home…just take him in the bedroom, if he wants to go…."

At Abbey's birthday party, I shared an intimate moment with Susan's parents after I ventured over to snap their photograph. Susan had rounded everyone up on their lush green lawn, for one-legged races, followed by a water balloon toss between parent and child. Susan was in her glory as the game captain, shouting out orders to her two brothers, Ed and John, their wives, Kathy, her sister, and all her nieces and nephews. The only thing missing was a whistle around her neck. Her parents were seated in the shade of a towering tree, holding hands under the pines, proudly watching their very healthy and active family enjoy life.

When I walked over to them with my camera, Mrs. Harris was now standing in front of her husband of more than 55 years. She held his hands, extended out like a child learning to "dance." Gone was the blank, distant stare from her husband's eyes. She was lovingly gazing into her husband's face, and he was grinning back at her. They were swaying as she held his outstretched hands, dancing as she sang every word to "Let me call you sweetheart...." From a respectful distance, I was privileged to share this sacred moment between them. The nurses had taught him to dance. In his early years he was a very handsome man and quite a ladies' man. For one passing moment, he was still that handsome guy. It was a precious moment between two sweethearts that I will never forget.

Did I mention Susan's delicious food buffet? Unfortunately, I was only on week two of the South Beach Diet that Susan raved about during our long dinner conversation. Motivated by all her weight-loss testimonies of friends, who lost big-time, I started the next day. After a 9 1/2-pound weight loss in the first two weeks, I was determined not to cheat. But, boy was I tempted by Susan's elaborate buffet. There was corn pudding casserole, rave review pasta salad (my recipe, but improved upon by Susan), deviled eggs, fruit-salad, cooked-down green beans, Don's secret-marinade sliced flank steak, Italian style chicken (my husband instructed me to get the recipe) and for the dieters – sugar free Jell-O salad, that no one ate, including me.

There was, of course, a beautifully frosted and delicious carrot sheet cake (so everyone said) topped with a Number Two candle. I noticed that someone cut a piece of the cake before the candle was lit and presented to Abigail. Fortunately for them, Susan didn't catch them in the act.

# "Cooking Isn't My Thing..."

"**P**lease let me bring something," coaxed Carol. I conceded, since she and her husband, Darrell, were bringing their out-of-town houseguests to our upcoming Easter Sunday fare.

Even though Carol, a health food guru, often comments, "Cooking isn't my thing," I really never thought she was serious about not cooking. However, that completely changed on that following Easter Sunday brunch in my home.

Determined to convert her husband to healthier eating habits at the office, Carol once packed Darrell a healthy deli-sandwich containing just kale and avocado. After work that evening, he came roaring through the door with demon fire in his eyes.

"Carol, don't ever pack me a ridiculous health food lunch like that again! That gross mess ended up in the trashcan! What on earth were you thinking?"

So, when Carol offered to "bring something" for my elegant buffet table, I couldn't chance that she might bring a salad with a mixed dressing concoction made of seaweed and turnip juice.

"Okay, why don't you bring a tossed salad with that delicious dressing that Jill served up last week?" I quickly suggested.

"Oh, good idea," Carol replied. " I'll call Jill for the recipe, and how about if I also bring a darling sheet cake with white frosting, green-coconut for grass and jelly beans for eggs."

"Oh! I saw a cake just like that at church when Karen

brought it in for the Elder's luncheon last Sunday. It was really adorable!"

"Yes!" exclaimed Carol, "That's where I got the idea. I'll call Karen for that recipe, too."

Easter brunch is far more hectic than any of our home fellowships, centered on good tasting food. Dashing off from church ahead of my guests requires a simple, uncomplicated menu and deliberate planning. But, all my devising during the pre-planning stage did not prepare me for the near disaster that followed those two borrowed recipes, prepared by a friend who often claims, "Cooking isn't my thing!"

The night before my party, after an exhilarating day of cleaning and cooking, I stood back beaming at the beautiful setting I joyfully had created. Looking forward to serving our twelve dinner-guests the next day, my dining room table glistened with rose-tinted stemware, and silver-rimmed, white Lenox dishes. The silk flower centerpiece looked stunning atop the pink brocade tablecloth. A place card for each guest was elegantly written in calligraphy, propped up by an inexpensive porcelain gift box full of exquisite, foiled covered chocolate eggs.

Martha Stewart would have been proud of me.

Earlier Saturday evening, when I called Carol for the precise spelling of her friend, "Gayle Ann," a glamorous gospel singer, married to Jim, the visiting couple from Nashville, Carol sounded exasperated.

"Right now, I am over here dealing with the current disaster for the day," she bemoaned, but managed to laugh. "Frosting leaked out all over the inside of my refrigerator, out the bottom and down on the floor.

And to top it off, our guests are due to arrive any minute!"

Fortunately, I didn't relate to "the frosting" as belonging to the cute little bunny cake being served, as the lone dessert, at my picture-perfect affair. I would have fretted about it.

God must have a sense of humor for those of us who pattern our somewhat pretentious style of serving by trying to measure up to Martha Stewart!

The next day, when Carol called on the way to our home, asking if I had any "tarragon" on hand, I still had no misgivings about her cooking competence. However, the Martha-in-me felt compelled to comment. "Carol, if you mix the oil up with the herbs and spices the day before, it will taste better."

Since Carol and party were late leaving church, it gave me additional time for pleasurable, last minute primping around the house. Valuable time, I should have used to pray for "the test" that was soon to follow that afternoon at my house.

My beautiful buffet table was laden with honey-baked ham, sliced turkey breast, scalloped potatoes, baked beans, fruit salad, green beans, and yeast rolls – all prepared from scratch.

A few weeks earlier, when Carol learned of the traditional menu, she laughed. "My husband is going to be so thrilled! Just this morning, Darrell had just been begging for 'ham' right before you called to invite us to your down-home buffet!"

When our special guests finally arrived, Carol handed me a platter of messy sponge cake, hacked up into uneven squares, dotted with just one or two token jellybeans.

"Well," she said with a chuckle, handing off the botched up sheet-cake. "This is what's left of it after the frosting ran off on to my kitchen floor."

Thank God I took out that homemade banana-peanut butter-chocolate pie in the freezer as a back up, I thought, graciously taking the disastrous dessert from her hands. At least Carol's salad greens looked fresh, ready to be tossed with Jill's delicious dressing recipe, minus the fresh tarragon.

"This dressing is really supposed to be put in a blender," Carol calmly remarked, as she leisurely began to re-assemble the dressing ingredients from her carry-in containers. With the swiftness of a drill sergeant, I jerked open a drawer to accommodate her.

"Hey, I've got the perfect thing – a Christmas gift and I haven't used it yet. TV Emeril calls it his boat motor," I remarked, trying to sound cheerful to mask my impatience.

After plugging it in, Carol stuck the slender hand-held, blender-gadget in the narrow plastic cup containing the dressing and pushed the switch. The motor sounded tired, laboring to beat the dressing, so I leaned over to take a peek.

"Hmmm…why is that dressing so thick?" I asked, wondering why it resembled wet cement.

"Well," said Carol, "It called for three and a half cups! I told Jill 'that just couldn't be right' when I took the recipe down over the phone. I asked her three times, but she insisted it called for three and a half cups of sugar!"

Realizing Jill actually meant "one third to a half cup of sugar," without a word of Martha-mode-correction, I fetched my favorite olive oil dressing from the fridge. Then, I swiftly scooped out a tablespoon of the granulated glue to shake together in the bottle, before pouring it over the now droopy salad greens.

At the dinner table, Carol's husband entertained us all by reliving the night before.

"Carol, what's this all over the kitchen floor?!"

"Hmmm? What's the matter, Darrell? Is the refrigerator leaking water?" responded Carol, absentmindedly, glancing up from reading her Bible while seated in the living room.

"Carol, refrigerator's don't leak maple syrup! You better get in here right away."

During those first few moments of catastrophic discovery, I telephoned with my calligraphy pen in hand. As Carol was spelling out "Gayle Ann," the doorbell rang.

Later, at my party, the Martha in me had to get to the bottom of the cake fiasco. Carol explained. Being a "junk-free" household, she had used up the sole bag of granulated sugar on the salad dressing. Later, when the frosting recipe for the cake called for "granulated" sugar to fold into the stiff egg whites, all Carol could find on the shelf was fine "powdered" sugar. It whipped up to a nice, stiff rich icing. She happily decorated the frosted cake with green coconut flakes and carefully placed colorful jelly beans all about. However, the icing soon went limp and rolled down off the cake within minutes after being placed in the refrigerator!

Yet, in spite of all my "Martha" attempts for perfection, Easter feast tasted delicious. But more importantly, the Christian fellowship was far better. God has ways of humbling me, reminding me that our Lord Jesus Christ is the express purpose of our gatherings – not the food, nor the decorations or the fancy linen napkins that perfectly coordinate with the table covering. Come to think of it, Carol seldom gets uptight about anything. Like Mary, she is so often at the feet of Jesus in prayer or meditating on God's Word. My dear, cheerful friend makes everyone around her feel at ease, loved, and accepted – a valuable lesson, worth learning even if "cooking isn't her thing." In addition to the Word of God, Carol also challenges us to chew on vitamin rich stuff, like kale whenever possible.

# Preferential Treatment

I have to admit my two Boxers are spoiled rotten. Whenever I warm up their dog food in the microwave, my husband often teases them. "In my next life, I want to come back as one of your mom's dogs!" Or he'll add, "Those dogs get better medical treatment than me and they never miss a meal."

My beloved dogs are my constant companions whenever possible. Shortly before I amble around the house hunting down my purse and shoes they become anxious to "go bye-bye" in the car with me. Time and weather permitting they travel to the bank, to the grocery, and on other short excursions around town. When it's frigid weather they wear warm coats. They become frenzied when I allow them to come with me, but they will hold perfectly still for the fleece-lined coverings to be Velcro-ed together to stay on their backs.

Once I open the back door of my car, Zoey, the alpha female, will always nudge Peetie out of the way for the front passenger seat while dutiful Peetie remains banished to the back. After I exit the car, Zoey will jet behind the wheel, to sit perfectly erect in my seat, until I return. One time as I was coming out of a pet store, to enter my car, I heard someone laugh. The man passing by said, "He looks like your chauffer."

One summer evening, while I was in my local supermarket, a sudden downpour hit, but I forgot the dogs were in the car with the sunroof open. It was a gusher and the poor things were huddled together in the back seat completely drenched. It was the first time Zoey ever lowered her status to join Peetie in the backseat. I apologized profusely and when they got home, I gave them each a warm bubble bath.

A few days ago, I left my two honeys in my car to run into the corner drug store. I was able to find a parking spot right in front of the entrance. A happy-go-lucky African-American Salvation Army representative was dressed in a Santa outfit ringing his bell for donations. We exchanged a friendly greeting as I passed him to enter the store. I intended to print a few pictures to frame for last minute Christmas gifts, but the line was too long at the self-serve, print-your-own pictures machine. Just as I made the decision to go elsewhere I heard the blaring noise of a car-alarm gone off. I had a sinking suspicion that it was my car. Sure enough, my car lights were blinking on and off to the beat of the horn blasts. As I rushed past Santa I asked, "What happened? Did someone bump the car?" Santa seemed delighted to tattle on my naughty dogs.

"Nope," he said, pointing his finger, "it was those two." He snickered. "And they knew it was wrong because they stopped barking as soon as the alarm went off. And it was him in the front seat who triggered it."

As I quickly jerked open the door to stop the alarm by a keyless gizmo in my purse I said, "Well, she acts like a him, but they're actually two girls."

My son and husband love it that Zoey is very aggressive. I don't think it's cute at all, so I favor Peetie because she was a pound rescue. Her name is Petra, but I affectionately call her Peetie or Sweet Pea. One of my friends observed the two dogs together. She said to me, "You need to call that one "petrified" instead of Petra because she's so frightened of everything." Therefore, aggressive Zoey does all the begging for the two of them while I'm munching on snacks in front of the TV. With bold, probing eyes, Zoey will keep staring at me long after the popcorn or pretzels are polished off. It doesn't matter that the Vet scolds me whenever they gain a pound or two.

# My Dogs Love Godiva
# White Chocolate

Our adult twin daughters spent some time here during their Christmas break from work. We were surrounded by holiday goodies, but I felt guilty munching on something the dogs couldn't share with us. Naturally the fudge brownies and homemade chocolate chip cookies were a no-no for the dogs.

In addition to their full times jobs, both my hard-working daughters obtained part-time seasonal jobs to supplement their income. Elisa worked at a posh Godiva chocolate shop in Easton Town Center, an exclusive shopping center here in Columbus. Only the rich and famous can afford to shop there. With her employee discount Elisa rewarded us with an elaborate box of divine, but very expensive, assorted dark and milk chocolates. Tonight, while watching a Hallmark movie, I carefully held up each chocolate morsel to consider eating. Over the years I've been notorious about punching in the back of a chocolate and putting the disappointment back in the box. I knew better with this expensive assortment. Before tasting I asked Elisa about the center ingredient inside.

It wasn't long before Zoey got a whiff and stood peering at me with pleading eyes. Then I remembered my dog biscuit recipe book: White chocolate is safe for dogs. I was delighted to discover four pieces of white chocolate among the assortment, which I lovingly divvied up for Zoey and Peetie to eat. Elisa laughed at me.

I smiled at my dogs because they became instantly alert and waiting for more. I spoke a solemn truth to them by saying, "I hope you realize that you're probably the only two boxers in American history who have ever eaten imported Godiva chocolate."

Between the five of us, girls, we managed to nearly finish off the entire box of Godiva while watching the movie. The only three pieces left were undesirables – a chocolate covered cherry, a flat, mint-filled wafer, and a solid bittersweet chocolate star.

My chocolate-lover husband wandered through the living room about an hour later. He headed straight toward the Godiva. He lifted the gold-foil lid, expecting to find the same assortment from an hour earlier. "Boy, you three sure managed to eat all these chocolates in a hurry," he said, with exasperation.

I didn't dare tell him there were actually five of us in the mix.

# Intervention

As youngsters, my Aunt Kate and her younger sister Margaret played the highly addictive game of Jacks every chance they got from sunup to sundown. Eating, riding bikes, or doing chores was secondary to the driving force of tossing that little red, rubber ball in the air and snatching up the small, galvanized metal, six-tip objects in a pre-ordained and sequential system starting with "onesies," then "twosies," and so on. The set was ten Jacks. Variations included "double bounces," "pigs in the pen," "over the fence," "eggs in the basket," "flying Dutchman," and "around the world," to name just a few.

Even though Margaret was five years younger than Kate, she was quickly recruited as a substitute Jacks partner at home when sister wasn't playing with her girlfriends in the 8th grade. If the teacher left the classroom for a few minutes, Kate and Mary McGrath lunged to the floor for a quick fix. They managed a speedy few rounds before the unsuspecting teacher returned. That required a lookout at the classroom door to give fair warning when the teacher approached, which, like all addictions, added another elicit element of suspense.

Kate most likely was the compulsive Jacks reigning champion at school because she threw herself, whole-heartedly, into everything she did throughout her entire life.

My grandparents, John "Cecil" and Elsie Lambert, spent every Saturday doing their weekly errands of grocery shopping and visiting her mother, my great-grandmother Lydia Brant for tea and a bite to eat. Kate could count on them being gone several hours to spend her Saturday afternoon playing Jacks, non-stop, with Margaret.

The girls were given chores to complete before their parents returned home. However, they played jacks until Grandpa's car was spotted coming down the street. They'd hide the evidence and jump into action—making beds, washing and drying breakfast dishes, sweeping floors or dusting for their mother. While playing Jacks on the floor, there was no official lookout, so they resorted to taking quick, systematic, sneak peeks out the bay window between dramatic tosses of the metal jacks spilling across the dining room oak floor.

One infamous Saturday, the girls were so absorbed in throwing jacks that they didn't hear the car pull into the driveway. Not a single chore had been done. When Cecil came into the messy kitchen and caught them playing Jacks he was furious. He angrily scooped up the Jacks and the little red, rubber ball and stormed out the back door of their Cape Cod style home. With all his might grandpa threw the ball and Jacks high into the air over the backyard. Before the Jacks hit the grass, to be lost forever, a holy hush fell on the girls, who didn't dare protest, because they had been royally busted. As dutiful daughters, they trailed off to complete their chores in sullen silence.

Later, my kind-hearted grandfather most likely made an attempt to retrieve the Jacks. Kate certainly must have tried before going through de-tox with the most effective intervention in the history of all compulsive, childhood addictions to date!

# Tough Acts to Follow

I'm fortunate to have been influenced by a long line of admirable women who are artistic, fun loving, and hospitable.

As a young child, my great Auntie Colleen was my first role model. My mom and I were frequent guests at her table since we lived a few blocks away from the home of my great grandmother, Lydia Brant, and her youngest daughter, Colleen. I don't remember what delicious food Auntie probably served, but I vividly remember how special I felt. The amber colored stemmed goblets sitting on pretty placements with matching cloth napkins dazzled me. I became a princess.

When first married, living in Centerville, Ohio, my good friend Maggie often came to my aid. She was chock-full of brilliant ideas to send my way. I could always count on her for creative party favors and scrumptious ways to serve food. In her early career, marvelous Maggie was an interior decorator so even her clothes closet was color-coded, neat as a pin and aesthetically arrayed like a scene from Better Homes & Gardens. She told a tale on herself that gave me hope. One early morning the doorbell rang. She staggered to the door in her nightgown, hair a mess and still groggy from rolling out of bed. It was a scheduled home visit with her son's fourth grade teacher that she'd completely forgotten about!

In junior high school, home economics, the late Barbara Hutto was another tremendous encouragement to me. This outstanding teacher taught her young students to sew and cook, but it was her fascinating stories that made our class time so enjoyable.

One summer Barbara's dad assigned a list of very important things his teenage daughter needed to accomplish before the summer came to an end. Practical skills he felt all women needed to learn to do, such as changing the oil in an automobile, changing a spare tire and cooking a chicken dinner from "scratch." However, "scratch" in those days meant that she first had to catch the chicken, wring its neck, then chop off its head on a wood stump before plucking out all the feathers in time for supper. Chuckling, Mrs. Hutto confessed that her father never caught on that her boyfriend saved the day on the chicken stew. Since hearing that repulsive story early in life, I've never served another piece of fried chicken without thanking Jesus for skinned poultry parts, already assembled in grocery store packages!

In my early years of marriage, those countless, step-by-step, illustrated cookbooks were a source of salvation until the messianic-like ascension of Martha Stewart on the scene. Our girl enlightened us. She inspired us with stuff we never learned on our own or in a home economics class!

Perhaps it was that early childhood, "I feel-like-a-princess," experience that causes me to set out my fancy stemmed glassware and to never pass up a bargain-buy on placemats with matching napkins for every meal. I treat my family and friends like royalty when they dine at my table. Some people might consider that "puttin' on the dog," but so what if you get bit in the process?

If we never risk trying out new or slightly complicated recipes, we end up with those same, run-of-the-mill, standby meals that end with "helper." Or we resort to the unimaginative greasy, fried meals our mothers and grandmothers faithfully cranked out, like clockwork, from their trusty cast-iron skillets. Now those tasty, down-home dishes are very comforting following a funeral but not for a healthy way of life.

So, ladies, here's "puttin' on the dog" to you and your daughters from here on. And I sure hope you never get bit!.

From left: Elsie Brant Lambert, my grandmother, Lydia Margaret Powless Brant, my great grandmother, me as a baby, my mother, Shirley Lambert Taylor. Detroit, Michigan 1948.

*Lydia Margaret (Powless) Brant is a direct descendant of George Croghan, (1718-1782) a prominent Irish colonist, Onondaga Council sachem, land specula, and British Indian agent in colonial America.*

*His daughter, Catherine Croghan, married Chief Thayendanega (Joseph Brant), an influential Mohawk military and political leader closely associated with Great Britain during and after the American Revolution.*

*As a dedicated Christian, Mohawk Chief Joseph Brant translated the Book of Matthew, the Acts of the Apostles and the Book of Prayer into the Mohawk language to further advance the Gospel of Jesus Christ.*

*The matriarch Turtle Clan of this Canadian Mohawk tribe has produced architects, physicians, chiropractors, pharmacists, teachers, engineers, marketing professionals, musicians, artists, and authors as dedicated Christians who carry on the legacy of Chief Joseph Brant.*

*My mother's namesake, Aunt Shirley Brant McCoy, was the first Native American Indian to graduate from Michigan State University and not the last from our family.*

## Joseph Brant

*Joseph Brant or Thayendanegea was a Mohawk Indian leader and commanded Iroquois forces that fought for the British during the Revolutionary War. As a young man, Brant was befriended by the British and sent to school. He became a Christian and missionary among his people. Later in life he became a colonel in the British army and honored by the King and Queen of England with land in Canada. After the American Revolution, he moved to Canada and continued his missionary work.*

# Infamously Funny at Five

The first person I remember making laugh was Lydia Margaret Brant, my maternal great-grandmother. I was five-years-old.

One afternoon visit, while seated on a sofa, Grandma Brant contently gazed out the picture window while I secretly stared at her from across the room. I sat quietly on another couch studying everything about her. Her wavy, white hair with a twinge of purple was neatly combed off her sturdy face, complimenting her prominent beak. Wearing a light bluish-gray dress, her neck was adorned with proper pearls.

"Is it true you're a full-blooded Indian?" I asked hesitantly, my eyes narrowing with genuine suspicion.

"Yes, I am," she announced proudly with a twinkle in her eye.

"Well?" I said, shrugging my shoulders, "where are all your feathers?"

I wasn't trying to be funny, but she threw her head back to release a hearty, gut level howl. I didn't crack a smile because I had no idea why she was laughing so hard.

I've been told that my grown son, Robert Alexander, "Bo," and I've inherited the "Brant sense of humor," although my dad embarrassed us kids by laughing the loudest in the movie theatre back in the day when Tom and Jerry cartoons accompanied every feature film. Now, I am just as guilty as laughing the loudest at something profoundly ridiculous.

Authors are instructed to find their "voice" in writing. It needs to come through as genuine and true. When I began recording these downhome stories, I discovered my funny bone, something I didn't realize I had until it emerged in written form.

Hopefully, these light-hearted confessions will also strike a silly chord within you, as well. It's a pleasure to share them with you now.

# Sewing Club

Sewing Club was a monthly event for the women in the Brant-Lambert family. The ladies took turns hosting with a delicious dessert following a few hours of giddy gab. Family updates and concerns were discussed in detail. In addition, creative recipes were tested out during the time when Betty Crocker was the reigning queen of cookbooks. Not much actual sewing happened, although I do remember Aunt Bev and Auntie Colleen knitting non-stop whenever the group gathered in our home. A rotating treasurer collected fifty-cent dues in a glass jar full of quarters, nickels and dimes.

Aunt Margaret often recalls stories from this bygone era. She is a natural storyteller, so I've relied on her memory to keep these humorous stories alive.

Since the drawing power of these gatherings was the fellowship they shared, the other component was food. However, getting ten women seated around a table to eat was certainly a challenge. Makeshift table extenders were often a creation of one or two card tables added to a dining-room table, so finding enough chairs was an added burden. But, by hook or crook, they managed.

Naturally, the aspiration of each hostess was to serve a knock-um-dead dessert to impress. Believe it or not, pineapple upside-down cake had a place of origin in American history. I can well imagine that when Aunt Bev first served this fancy Betty Crocker dessert rage it brought ooos and ahhs from the ladies. But, unless you knew not to slice out an entire pineapple ring, the huge cake portion was enough to feed two hungry men. Aunt Bev sat down after dishing up the last humungous plate of pineapple upside-down cake, dotted with a red cherry in the center of the pineapple ring and topped with a dollop of fresh whipped cream. Everyone anxiously waited for the gracious hostess to get situated before diving into the hungry-man size helping. Margaret glanced around the table. Dorothy, a petite woman, five-foot standing, was seated on a piano bench that was about four inches lower that the other chairs. Her nose was level with the gigantic cake creation that towered above her head! The poor thing needed to be sitting on a couple of phone books to be seen!

Another origin in American history was a restaurant offering open pit grilling. One evening the Sewing Club members were returning from a social outing. Something they did in addition to their in home fellowships. Since an open grill hamburger was such a brand new concept, they stopped in at the Dix Open Pit Barbeque Grill located on Dix Road.

Naturally, a group that size was a delight to the chef because the place was near empty when the club strolled in. The young waitress eagerly wrote down their burger orders and soon returned with a large tray of ice cold drinks. Within minutes the place erupted with the shrieks of terror from the ten club members who bolted from their chairs. On cue, the waitress appeared holding a broom while sauntering over to wild-eyed group huddled together by the edge of the table.

"Where is he?" She spoke in a calm, nonchalant voice as if the mouse running back and forth on the window ledge made a nightly debut.

The terrified women fled for their lives as if a bomb had exploded in the kitchen. "As we rushed past the open pit grill, I glanced at those ten burgers loudly sizzling as the chef flipped them with glee." Margaret said.

The year my teenage mother was elected treasurer of the Sewing Club brought on another hearty chuckle from my aunt's treasury of humorous events. The quarters accumulated each month for club dues added up to about sixty bucks by the end of the year. In those days, it was enough cash for the ladies to take their husbands out on the town. I can imagine how my mother's face dropped when a dinner at a fancy restaurant was planned for the next month. All year, she had been dipping in the kitty when no one was looking. A quarter in those days probably bought a loaf of bread, a gallon of milk and a pack of smokes. In my parents early years of married life my hard working dad managed by living paycheck to paycheck with no complaints.

Nothing was said throughout dinner after the ladies and partners ordered up eighteen medium-rare steaks. My dad had to foot the bill but not without a tattling on my mother. She said, "What do you mean? I saw you dipping into those quarters, too!"

Sewing Club marched on for many more years. Mom was never again elected treasurer; the ladies never again graced the door of Dix Open Pit Barbeque and no actual sewing was ever accomplished.

But fun memories live on in the hearts of those who made the effort for the sake of just being together.

# Mom and Me Are Now
# Senior Citizens!

*December 7, 2008*

*Dear Mom,*

*Here we are honoring you on your 80th birthday year with all the "cousies" and aunties at our annual Christmas party.*

*Who'd ever think we'd be sitting together, one day, reminiscing as "senior citizens?" When I was eleven years old, I can vividly remember when you were getting ready to turn thirty. You kept threatening to hang a black wreath on our front door as a sign of mourning.*

*In many ways we grew up together. You missed out on so much in life by getting married so young, so I am especially grateful for the sacrifices you made on my behalf.*

*Some of my fondest memories were of you trying to get me, David, and Dennis up in the morning for "school-dazies." I am quite certain that I was the hardest to wake up since I always stayed up late as the big night owl. In fear of having me arise crabby and hateful, you relied on special tricks like sending Suzette, our pampered poodle, into my room to leap on my head and zealously lick my face awake. Or you'd put one of your favorite albums on the stereo and crank it up full volume to arouse us out of a coma. I remember awakening many a morning to Broadway hits or Joni James, Harry Belefante, or*

*Johnny Mathis crooning away at the crack of dawn. If that didn't work, as a last resort, you'd take a broom handle and pound the ceiling below my bedroom floorboard. But the broom trick wasn't used very often because I surely would end up in a foul mood for the day.*

*Right out of high school I remember applying for a job with Bell Telephone Company. The application had a space that requested information regarding my high school attendance record with a check mark for "times absent." I called home, confident that you'd confirm that I certainly had "good attendance." You said, "Are you kidding? You were absent just about every Monday."*

*Suzette was so full of personality. You loved Bun candy bars: Round with a maple filling and a chocolate and peanut covering. I don't think they make them anymore. Whenever you unwrapped your Bun bar, that crazy poodle would come flying out of nowhere to yip up and down for a bite. In those days, no one warned us not to give chocolate to dogs, and they all survived anyway. You never liked sharing your beloved Bun bar, so to enjoy eating in peace, you'd have to sneak upstairs to climb in bed, under the covers, so the dog wouldn't hear the unwrapping. You went to great length to keep her radar ears from hearing the paper tear open. And if you weren't quick enough, she'd start digging at the covers to expose your sin.*

*When you lived here in Columbus for a couple of years, you sometimes babysat for wealthy families, and they all adored you. One time you were babysitting for some kids, and another candy-loving toy poodle of yours got into an Easter basket and ate up all the candy. That darn dog became so bloated that she remained stuck up on the bed, next to the Easter basket, unable to jump back down. You probably called her, "Faaatsooo," even though she was aptly named "Candy."*

*One night, a few days after we moved to Waverly Street, you rushed into my bedroom and flipped on the bright overhead light. Without shutting off the light, you jumped in bed with me and jerked the covers over our heads, like a kid hiding from the Boogie Man. The way you were shaking I thought a burglar had broken into the house. I was nine-years old. I got frightened and asked, "What's wrong?"*

*You said, "There's a MOUSE on the loose!" Actually, I could go on and on about several famous mouse stories through the years growing up with a Mother terrified of mice.*

*Mom, I appreciate all of your delicious home cooked meals and your pleasant disposition while caring for us. I often heard you humming, whistling, or singing while you worked around the kitchen. I also think you knew every nursery rhyme under the sun. When that hit television show called "Name That Tune" hit the airwaves, you always beat out the actual contestants by naming the tune after three or four notes. You were truly amazing. You were also my dictionary throughout school. If I was writing something I'd yell out, "Hey Mom, how do you spell 'appreciation'?" Without a beat you'd yell back "a-p-p-r-e-c-i-a-t-i-o-n." I don't think you were ever stumped. I truly do appreciate you with more fond memories than anything else.*

*Your sense of humor is legendary, and, of course, you loved to tease everyone to death. You made us laugh till we were breathless by your witty, off-the-wall remarks. I sincerely regret that I didn't record some of them. So, right now I am relying on my memory that is getting more distant as the years fly by.*

*But I do remember one, funny, comment you made in the presence of a classmate. That comment became legendary. In junior high, my chum, Carol Ellstrom, and I were with you getting gassed up at a service station in that famous Pink Thunderbird of yours. That was in the day when gas station attendants actually filled your tank, wiped your windshields, front and back, cleaned off your side-view mirrors, and lifted the hood to check your oil level and didn't expect a tip. The man performing this amazing service was a big, burly guy who was on the homely side. After he walked away, you let out a one-liner that said it all. You quipped, "Hoommeer." I thought Carol was going to convulse because she was laughing so hard. From that point on "homer" became the official byword among our classmates. Anyone who was a "big homer" was called "homeroo, homeretta or homeretski, this referring to someone who looked, dressed, or acted funny. And trust me, many days I look and feel like a big homer when I look in the mirror.*

*Mom, I think you were the happiest serving others, going out of your way to help a family member or someone in desperate shakes. Dennis' friends all camped out like refuges in your basement at one time or another. David and I get it honest, because our homes have always been open to a wayward teen or distant cousin finding roost.*

*Cousin Linda lived with us for about two years, right before she married Tommy. The last time we were together, which was your 75th birthday, Linda had me cracking up over the notorious tales that went on in our home, especially with Dad, who was her "Uncle Guy." She quoted some of Uncle Guy's infamous notes he wrote before leaving for work. For instance, one morning Dennis' rotting tennis shoes were plunked down on the kitchen table with a note. It read, "Please leave in the back yard to FUMIGATE."*

*Another time, I left a note on the kitchen table to remind the family that we needed to be on the watch to "collect a fresh stool from Suzette to take to the vet today." Dad came along and added, "Don't worry...plenty of fresh ones in basement."*

*Linda thought our family was just the greatest, liberated household on earth because her strict, Italian father, our Uncle Guido, was too uptight about everything, which is probably why she ended up living with us during high school. We all loved Linda, didn't we? Like her mother, my dear Aunt Ruth, Linda died way too soon.*

*Dearest Mother, I thank you for your loving nature and generous spirit that kept our family close. I will always treasure Dad's South Carolina family connections "down south" and the Michigan Lambert/Brant family gatherings "up north" that remain so very important to me.*

*Last summer when you and I were together at Aunt Claire's cottage up north, I cherish that intimate time we had remembering our Dennis. His sudden death caught everyone by surprise. We both shed some needed tears and expressed our deep sorrow for my baby brother. We didn't get a chance to do that at his memorial service with so many people around, so I am glad we had that tender moment alone, remembering our "Dean." He was such a character. At the memorial service his Ann Arbor friends all had endearing things to say about him like he was their hero. I am so grateful to the Lord that my brother had many friends who dearly loved him, too.*

*I am very happy that you have Tom in your life and that you're not alone in your golden years. Tom has remained very devoted to you all these years following Dad's death and the stroke that has left you unable to communicate very well. I know that you appreciate all the sacrifices that Tom makes on your behalf. He's a great guy with a big tender heart just like yours. It always blesses me when I see both of you with tears in your eyes over something sentimental. God bless you, always. I hope and pray that you and Tom have many more years together in good health with peace of mind.*

*Authors Note: My mother suffered an aneurism in 1993 and he is no longer able to speak very well. However, she understands everything and hasn't lost her ability to laugh at a good joke, hum a tune, or play the organ. My tribute letter was read at a Christmas party to honor her 80th birthday.*

# Baby Boomer Hair Disasters

As I slid into the booth joining my Aunt Bonnie and her best friend for lunch, I commented on the cute, but rather odd, hat perched on Marie's head. The twosome were already seated at Applebee's waiting for me to join them.

"I only have this hat on to cover the worst haircut of my life," Marie moaned.

That innocent comment unleashed a litany of past hairdo mishaps stored within our vaults for such a time as this.

My mother's baby sister, Bonnie, turned to me with glee, about to share something funny. We grew up together since she is only three years older than I. "Do you remember the time my sister, Marilyn, put on a ball cap hat but her bangs went way past her nose, so she trimmed them back using the edge of the hat as a guideline?" I actually hadn't heard that infamous Lambert family story. "When she took off the hat her bangs had shrunk up to the edge of her scalp."

Without missing a beat, Marie chimed back in. "Oh! When I was little, one time my mother cut my bangs so short they stuck straight off my forehead like an umbrella for weeks!"

That triggered a response from my memory bank. "Do you remember the popular Dorothy Hamel haircut from the 1980s?" I asked, my laughter finally subsiding to explain why. That ice skater's short, side feathered bob led to a longer version for all the little girls across America. The hairstyle was feathered to look like Dorothy on the side of the head but the remaining hair was shoulder length. "When the twins were about six years old, I attempted to feather their hair in front of their ears, but I cut it on the wrong angle and really botched it up. I took them to a professional hair stylist explaining what happened. As the beautician led my girls away she said, 'So, you just want me to even up their hair with the length on the sides, right?' I remained in the waiting room reading magazines thinking they were in good hands. An hour later, Elisa and Leanne returned to me with half-inch pixie cuts. They were nearly scalped."

Hairdo nostalgia continued as our huge appetizer sampler arrived. Ben, our waiter, couldn't figure out why we were laughing each time he came to refill our iced tea glasses. I recalled the ancient days before the invention of curlers and curling irons. "Remember when our mothers used long strips of rags to wrap our hair into Shirley Temple curls?" It was time to confess my first sin of covetousness. In the second grade I sat behind Rose Mary who had luscious long curls with colorful ribbon bows that always matched her darling dresses. Her thick, luscious hair had a 'natural' wave, so all her Italian mother had to do was wrap each long strand of hair around her finger to create an even row of plump sausage curls that never went straight and limp like my skimpy curls did. My little seven-year-old heart yearned with envy over those gorgeous curls day after day. She was also the teacher's pet. Therefore, our schoolmarm with the short fuse never yelled at Princess Rose Mary.

Our teacher was a tyrant and often grabbed fellow

students, usually rambunctious boys, by the shoulders to shake the liver out of them. One day, our class lined up, by the exit-door, single file, anxious for recess. That day, Rose Mary was caught in the cross fire of our teacher's wrath. In secret glee, I watched those devilish curls fly back and forth around her head because she had never been singled out, as the rest of the class had been scolded that entire year. Sadly, that's the only thing I remember about second grade. That, and a boy named Michael who was so terrified by our wicked teacher that he left a puddle under his desk one afternoon, too afraid to ask to use the restroom. Neither one of my fellow students probably ever recovered from the trauma.

Bonnie reminded us of bobby pins from the 1950's after rag curls were no longer in vogue. Two of my mother's five younger sisters, Kate and Margaret, were close in age. They each stored a fistful of bobby pins in their own teacup on my grandmother's hutch. Before bed each night, my aunts would "set their hair." This was achieved by wrapping several strands of hair around their finger in tight pin curls around their face, ideally using two bobby pins, crisscrossed, to hold the curled hair in place while sleeping. However, when the black bobby pins became scarce, the girls would resort to using only one bobby pin to hold the curl in place, which of course, wasn't as secure as the luxury of two.

One-night, Kate came home late from a date. She had to go to work the next day so it was imperative that she "set her hair" before going to bed. When she went to her teacup all her bobby pins were missing! She came into the bedroom to discover her younger sister snoring soundly with her hair set in tight pin curls, not just around her face but also all over her entire head using two bobby pins for each curl.

Kate was so angry that she began pulling the pins out of the sleeping culprit's curls. Margaret awakened and a "silent" fight broke out to keep from waking the entire household. They ended up on the floor of their clothes closet before my grandfather broke up the brawl.

When home perms came along, we all suffered from chemical over-kill. My poker-straight hair turned to frightening frizz after my mother zapped me the night before school photographs. My eighth-grade picture cured me of perms for about thirty years. Bonnie exclaimed, "Tell me about it! She did the same thing to me. I have a school picture with fuzz sticking straight out the sides of my Brownie cap!"

Just think of all the childhood anguish we could've been spared if the perm had never been invented and if we moms, the infamous kitchen beauticians, had only done what the Dads – determined, amateur plumbers, always did – leave it up to the professionals!

# Mechanical Giftedness
# Doesn't Run in Families!

When it comes to mechanical giftedness, I own the family toolbox. So, I know the essence of a drill bit when it comes to hanging pictures or installing curtain rods. On the other hand, my husband is not a Handy Andy, nor is he particularly interested in how mechanical things work. He knows the difference between a flat head and a Philips head screwdriver, but that's about it. Recently, to my surprise, I found a small hammer resting on the top of his armoire in the bedroom. I asked, "What's that hammer doing up there?"

"Because I can never find a hammer when I need one!" Daryl snapped.

I honestly don't remember him ever using a hammer the entire duration of our 30 plus years of marriage, so that's a new one on me. But at least I'll know where to find one in a pinch.

As a former Cadillac dealer, people were constantly asking Daryl advice about a chassis or other problematic car engine trouble, much like someone at a party sharing physical ailments with a guest doctor, who is trapped giving out free medical advice. Daryl was never able to give out mechanical counsel because he was completely clueless. Consequently, when our firstborn son married, I presented his wife with a fully equipped toolbox, as a bridal shower gift. My businessman stepson wasn't any more inclined to fixing things than his dad.

Last year, during the frigid month of January, late at night, I heard some loud banging noises because the temperature had dropped below zero. I instinctively knew it was water pipes freezing up. Before I went to bed, I left a note on the coffee pot for my husband to "check out the probability of frozen pipes somewhere in the house." (As if he'd know how.)

The next day, Daryl insisted that the banging I heard was just the wood on the deck expanding and contracting. Has anyone heard of that? Sure enough, a day later, our garage floor was flooded from two burst pipes. Our garage is plumbed for the bathroom in my husband's cozy two-room office located above the garage. The garage below needs to be heated for the living space above. A week before, my husband had "turned the heat down" in the lower garage space "to save on the gas bill." The money we paid a plumber to fix the pipes could have financed a trip to Hawaii for the winter.

But, in the past, I've been just as daft. Last summer I ventured to put a quart of oil in my car engine, all on my own – a first. After filling up my gas tank, I courageously entered the service station to purchase a quart of motor oil. However, the attendant helped me on what weight to purchase. After returning to my car, I located the release button to open the hood. I also figured out how to prop up the hood as well. I unscrewed the cap to the oil chamber, inserted the spout and emptied the entire can of oil into the well. I was feeling so proud of myself until I noticed an icon on the outside of the oil tank, which was a faucet with drips coming out of the water spout. I panicked because I had poured the oil into the water radiator! From my cell phone, I called my husband in tears. He immediately called the service department of a Cadillac dealership. He called back to tell me that the serviceman shouted, "Whatever you do, don't turn on the engine!" His outburst only added to my overall terror. Naturally, I dialed AAA emergency roadside service to have my car towed in. Within minutes Daryl arrived at the gas station to my rescue. When I sheepishly pointed out the hole where I had poured in the oil, he chuckled. Surprisingly, my husband knew that the new oil was in the right compartment after all.

I must confess that embarrassing incident has certainly made up for all the times I gloated about owning my own toolbox. Now I'm much more confident that I'll get to see my husband put his stashed hammer to good use in my lifetime! Wonders never cease

# Microwave Etiquette

Scraping off food spills and splatters inside a microwave oven is very irritating, especially if the previous users have not bothered to clean up their messes. I am speaking about the two adult males living in my home – my husband and our son.

About once every two weeks I end up taking out the large, round glass turn-about to wash it down in the kitchen sink. If the gravy or tomato drips have turned into hard, stuck-on scabs, it's a tough job. I usually resort to soaking the plate, one side at a time, in a soapy bath for hours. This is no small job.

On the last cleaning, I started to think about an alternative life style. For instance, what if the guilty parties had kindly taken a paper towel to blot up the spills as a courtesy to the next microwave user? Wow, think that one through for a moment with me. It would create less work for the chief cook, but more responsibility on the part of two kitchen stewards who cohabitate in the kitchen with me.

The first few days after a clean out, the microwaves sparkles each time you use it. It's rewarding to open the oven door to be greeted by a glistening clean oven. However, the first huge spill remains on the glass turntable unless someone cleans it up. If I don't come along to wipe it up while it's still wet, the spill becomes a permanent fixture because microwaves heat turns it into a crusty scab and probably just as deadly.

Soon, there are also grease splatters on the ceiling and sides mounting until it becomes a health hazard so gross that it's best to use a mask when I eventually break down to clean it out again. This cycle has gone on far too long. It's time to organize a national crusade against the slobs who refuse to conform.

On the last microwave flush out, I started to think about "microwave etiquette" and other courtesies that need to be instituted in the world. How about drips on the toilet seat? Or what about taking the last sheets of toilet paper without making provision for the next bare butt? At home, household members should always replace the empty roll. But in a public restroom, one should get a paper towel or some additional toilet paper from another stall to lie on the empty roll so the next person isn't panic-stricken. If that's not possible, notify the manager of the need. Common courtesy. Think ahead.

One time after getting lost and driving up to Pennsylvania instead of Ohio, we were a group of ditsy women traveling home from a church conference in Tennessee. We actually had a flip over Trip Tic from AAA, but still managed to get confused.

After traveling nine hours out of the way, Rebecca was the first one in the single bathroom at a gas station pit stop. It was about 2:30 a.m. and the lone attendant was busy with other customers. Rebecca hurried out of the unisex bathroom and looked around. "No toilet paper," she silently mouthed to those of us waiting in line. She dashed over to the coffee pot and grabbed some coffee filters as a last resort for toilet paper. We all followed suit with grateful hearts to Rebecca for having sense enough to provide an alternative to the empty toilet roll. Thinking ahead. It's all about consideration for the next person in line.

As I wrote that last paragraph, my husband had just come in from the grocery. He has been emptying a few grocery bags from the kitchen counter. Honest to God, he just called out to me in a singsong voice, "I got us toilet paper in the nick of time."

You have to admit that was a timely comment. We were both thinking along the same lines for a change.

Apparently, there are more courteous members in my family than I've given credit to. Since we seem to have the bathroom situation under control by the toilet paper commando, now I just need to instill new revelation concerning future microwave spills. I was thinking of a magnet that reads, "Take time to wipe."

# It Must Have Been the Drugs

Last summer my husband had a left knee replacement. Heavily medicated around the clock, Daryl had plenty of down time to watch NCIS reruns, bark orders, and analyze our household expenditures. That's how he began to obsess over our monthly trash bill.

Every resident in our small, quiet village needs to hire a private company to haul away household trash. After moving in, we connected with the "Flower" company that faithfully arrives every Tuesday in a mammoth, flowered purple truck.

For the past 15 years we've been "renting" two huge bins that hold a ton of trash. Apparently, the folks at Flower don't permit the outright purchase of these hefty tubs. They figure they'll find an absent-minded sucker on every block of customers who overlooks the rental rate.

One trash day, I arrived home to several over-stuffed plastic garbage bags piled high at the end of our driveway.

"I got rid of them," Daryl growled with a voice of triumph. "It's way too expensive."

I figured hubby was hallucinating from the around the clock pain meds the surgeon had prescribed. The drugs were obviously getting to him.

However, he had actually done the math on the trash bin rental and calculated we could own a beachfront condo for what we've paid out over the years.

I had no idea we were renting because I would've taken action long before then. Now caught up in a perpetual cycle of regret, Daryl was chomping at the bit to retaliate.

So off he went, that same afternoon, in 89-degree weather on an unauthorized medical post-surgery outing decked out in kaki shorts and donning heavy, thigh-high, white nylon stockings required for better blood circulation. He's a 6'5'' former offensive tackle for the NFL so he surely got plenty of gawks from fellow Lowe's shoppers that sweltering afternoon.

When Daryl got home he was giddy with excitement. "Boy, I've never done shopping that drew so much attention from other shoppers."

I tend to talk to everybody, but his reserved, melancholy temperament doesn't readily converse with strangers. "Really? What do you mean?" I asked, pretending to be oblivious to how ridiculous his long legs looked in those thick, white nylon stockings that went past his thighs and up under the edge of his shorts.

"Well, since they were priced by the gallon, I pulled out three different sizes to compare. While I analyzed the cost of each gallon another guy came along to purchase one. We discussed the price variations. The 32-gallon size was $16.98 and the 36-gallon size was $18.98. One had wheels and the other one didn't. He picked out the $16.98 without wheels and quickly left. I kept moving down the aisle and came across several larger sizes, so I also pulled them out to study. The biggest was a 95-gallon bin and cost $89.00. After I had about eight or nine bins lined up in the aisle a young couple stopped to watch."

I imagined the conversation went accordingly…

"Looks like you're in a project," she remarked, scanning the aisle crammed with bin after bin lined up like penguins waiting to take a plunge.

"Well, for 15-years I've been renting my trash bins for $7.00 a month," he grumbled. "It ticked me off so much, I felt like telling them to take their bins and shove it. At those prices they should be gold-plated." They surely wondered why it took him so long to come to that brilliant deduction.

When Daryl got outside with his newly purchased $89-dollar trash bin, he attempted to stuff the huge bin in the back seat of his Coupe Deville. Those long legs covered in white surely were a showstopper. An Indian woman, dressed in a colorful Sari, watched his struggle from across the parking lot.

In broken English she called out, "Why did you *buy* that? Don't you know that our city supplies free trash cans? If anything happens to the container you can just call and they come and replace it." She must have thought he hadn't been enlightened to the perks in the over-taxed suburb where that Lowe's store was located.

"Well, *where I live* I have to rent my bins," he bemoaned. Then, shaking his head, he added, "I didn't dare tell her how long I'd been renting. She stared at me with pity as it was."

Aside from those long legs in opaque white tights, resembling a Rockette in drag, in 90-degree heat, causing community commotion, this sudden surge of conversing with customers must have been the buzz he got from the drugs.

In any event, it was a pleasure hearing about his rare venture with complete strangers. What I wouldn't give to have a video of this played out on YouTube. It would have gone viral in minutes: Stunned Lowes Shoppers Spot Former OSU Offensive Tackle Sporting Tights While Examining Every Garbage Pail in Aisle Sixteen on Record Hot Day in Ohio.

# Senior Citizen's Squatter's Rights

For most of us, "a day at the beach" conjures up majestic images of sand castles, leisurely strolls collecting pretty shells, or body surfing on a cerulean blue shoreline with contrasting white sand.

Thirty-five pounds ago, and just about as many years, the photograph I cherish the most is of my Aunt Bonnie and me, close in age, lounging side-by-side in the surf in matching beach chairs barely inches off the ground. Our then tight, slender bodies were golden brown. Gentle waves from the Gulf of Mexico lapped at our feet as our kids frolicked in the surf nearby. Languishing there in the warm Florida spring sunshine, the echo of swirling seagulls in the distance sounded harmonic. Nothing seemed more idyllic than those tranquil times at the beach.

During a recent Florida vacation with my friend Katrina and her three-year-old son, Shem Josiah, we spent plenty of time and money at Wal-Mart. During one shopping spree I spotted two, low-slung beach chairs, reminiscent of my glory days and quickly placed them in my cart that also contained goggles, beach towels, beach ball, Styrofoam noodles and Shem's perfect size life jacket for the pool. But my preoccupied mind was filled with expectations of all the splendid moments we were going to have at the beach. I envisioned lounging on that low-slung chair with my legs stretched out in the water as our cute little boy calmly played in the tide with his little pail and shovel.

A week later, sunny weather permitting, we landed on the beach. However, I noticed that when I finally squatted down in my low beach chair to relax, it was the exact sensation of falling on my butt, a wee bit too scary for someone my age. I admitted nothing.

When it was time to get up I discovered that I was too far down on the ground to spring back up. Actually, without help, I could not lift myself out of the chair! I was mortified at the prospect of having to be assisted out of a lawn chair. How embarrassing! Did I really think I was still that the slim chick in the picture when I purchased those beach chairs designed for gymnasts? Thankfully I wasn't alone because I would have had resort to a military roll out onto the sand, then crawl to the study cooler for an anchor to brace myself up. Later, having to lay her cell phone down to use both hands, Katrina managed to pull me up.

During a recent conversation with my lifelong Canadian friend, Florence said something about side-by-side rocking lawn chairs on a deck overlooking mountains on Shawinigan Lake, British Columbia. She and her husband, Fred, recently relocated to this peaceful setting to continue retirement. As a former basketball player in college and woman's basketball coach, she's tall and still very athletic. The mention of lawn chairs triggered thoughts of that infamous day on the beach weeks earlier. She has a delightful sense of humor, so I confessed needing assistance out of the low beach chair. Naturally, we had a hearty laugh together. She said, "Oh, I know exactly what you mean! These days I have that same problem getting up from low toilets."

Now I am wondering why the taller baby boomers haven't protested by now. Along with a wheelchair stall in public restrooms, we also need higher toilet seats!

And as for those glamorous, low-slung beach chairs? There needs to be warning tag that reads: If you haven't been to the beach in twenty-five years, do not purchase this item. It will be hazardous to your ego!

# What Was I Thinking?

When my husband and I moved to Cape Coral, Florida, I was anxious to introduce my friend's three-old son, Shem Josiah, to the enchantment of "a day at the beach." This amazing child has become like a grandson to us. In anticipation of this bright and beautiful excursion, I purchased not one, but two complete sets of beach toys for the little boy who had never played in beach sand. This was done many months in advance. One sand play-set contained ingenious molds that actually reproduced ramparts, walls, towers, moats and drawbridges for castle authenticity. The other play-set featured a shovel, pail, trowel, strainer and nifty sea animal shapes to cast with moist sand. A huge red bucket held the various components for making the perfect sand castle in the sun.

When I grew up, all we had were our hands to dig, scoop and mold sand castles. We've come a long way!

Last Christmas, we beamed as the then two-year-old opened his numerous Christmas presents from all of us. When Shem unwrapped the elaborate sand castle molds he held the package up to ask: "What's this, Nana?" He seemed equally confused by my glowing explanation because he had never laid eyes on sand.

Seven months later, I couldn't wait to see the expression on his angelic face the first time he saw the sea. After peering around at the scantily clad-sunbathers, he quickly got in the spirit. He sat down to whip off his sandals to feel the warm sand between his toes.

During our late lunch at a beachside restaurant, I suggested he take a leftover French fry to "feed a seagull." While his mom remained in the restaurant, text-messaging a friend, Shem and I adventured down the weathered planks to the beach. He didn't quite understand the importance of holding the lone fry in the air. When a seagull flew overhead, I instructed him to toss it out to the sand. He laughed when the gull dove down to beak it before swallowing it whole. Fortunately we only had one French fry to share because a feeding frenzy would have erupted that would have surely frightened him.

Our beach day finally arrived during a sweltering week of 95-degree August weather. After three sweaty trips, Katrina, Shem's Mom and I lugged everything down to the sand in anticipation of an awesome day. Shem helped out by carrying his colorful beach towel. I brought some stale bread and cereal to feed the seagulls since Shem had giggled over the seagull coming so close to him on the previous beach visit. (Doesn't Martha Stewart always come prepared?)

After some strenuous grunt work, Katrina and Nana managed to secure the beach umbrella deep in the sand. I chided myself for not bringing a rawhide mallet. (Surely, Martha would have thought of bringing one.) In the shade of the umbrella, I placed the loaded down cooler between the two chairs now facing the water. I spread out the towels and slathered Shem down with sun block. I had stopped along the way to purchase another pair of pintsize sunglasses for him and some ointment for his lips. While his mother was twittering on her blackberry,

I finished setting up camp for "our fabulous day at the beach." We had enough food, snacks, cold soda, kiddie-size fruit drinks and suntan lotion to last an entire week. I even included a bottle of vinegar for the threat of a jellyfish sting. (Martha may not have thought of that one!)

Shem loved getting his feet wet because it felt like bath water. He had his life jacket on and his mother inched him in past his waist. Nowadays, I am ever aware of sharks, so I didn't go past my knees, but I said nothing of the potential hazard.

In the kitchen earlier that morning, peeling all those boiled eggs was a joy as I envisioned how hungry we'd be after spending the entire day on the beach. My homemade egg salad is Katrina's favorite, but later it was difficult to assemble sandwiches without getting sand on the bread. (What was I thinking?)

His mother and I briefly instructed Shem on the art of packing his colorful molds with just the right mix of water and sand to pat down, invert, admire and smash. He liked that. While his mother stepped away momentarily to retrieve another text message, I decided to perk things up. I produced the large bag of crumbs to feed the seagulls. It was a fateful decision.

The first two seagulls to land made Shem squeal with delight. However, within three seconds about fifty, screeching seagulls swarmed our space and Shem freaked out. He began screaming and, like a monkey, ran up his mother's leg for safety, clinging to her body for dear life. While balancing him on her hip Mom rushed him back in the water to escape the vulture-like swarm. It was a scene from Alfred Hitchcock's The Birds. She tried to coax her son down in the water but his legs curled up to his chest with terror. He was still screaming. (What was I thinking? I brought enough breadcrumbs for the entire Gulf coast!)

Not counting the twenty-plus minutes it took to unload the car and set up camp, our "day at the beach" lasted about seventeen minutes. After we re-loaded the trunk in the intolerable heat, we couldn't wait to get home to shower. We rode home in silence. What was I thinking?

We never returned to the beach. In fact, we never spoke of it, fearing Shem might need inner healing later in life. I had to admit that it was another clear case of putting on the dog, this time for a three-year-old, and not only getting bit, but nearly getting devoured by vicious seagulls in the process!

# High Expectations

It always happens when you least expect it. Disappointment. We start the morning off in a good mood then something goes haywire to ruin the day, if we let it. Expectations are usually lofty with some ideal in the center of our mind. Naturally, if our expectation is not met in the projected way, we become disappointed.

Recently, my Aunt Bonnie, friend Marie, and I were eating lunch on the veranda of a condominium golf course clubhouse that Bonnie now enjoys as an attractive bachelorette new resident. An hour earlier, I arrived at her condo with plans to spend a few relaxing hours at her pool following lunch. I entered her immaculately decorated condo with a pink noodle on one arm and my beach bag slung over my left shoulder. I wore a casual cover up over my bathing suit, Capri pants and dusty flip-flops. Bonnie opened the door decked out in full make up, lipstick, and highly scented-perfume wearing an outfit fit for New Year's Eve. Compared to how she was decked out, I felt like I just got out of a homeless shelter. Obviously, she had changed her mind about swimming. "Oh, it's too cold for the pool, don't you think?" she cooed.

"It's 79-degrees out," I sighed. "How hot does it need to be?"

At lunch us girls discussed the latest news. A few days earlier, Bonnie had orchestrated her second annual fundraiser

149

style show that took several months of creative planning. This year's zebra theme was done to precise perfection. The white linen covered tables had crystal-filled glass centerpieces containing a single, flaming red hibiscus flower. Generous merchant donations filled up countless raffle gift baskets, wrapped in clear cellophane like Easter baskets, tied in animal print ribbon. The volunteers, in all sizes, modeled the latest fashions from a high-end boutique.

And of course, the catered menu was as elegant. Bonnie said, "I used a new caterer this year. I told him that I wanted assorted bread in baskets, crusted gourmet breads, not those store-bought, spongy buns. He promised that each luncheon plate of salmon would be a beautiful presentation." I immediately gave her hand a celebrated high-five salute in praise of Martha Stewarts standard of excellence. She continued. "Well, when I finally sat down to eat, they served me this pitiful looking, tail-end of a very tiny, dry piece of salmon. I looked over at my co-chairman's serving and her dish looked like the cover of Gourmet magazine."

We've all been there. I recalled the time our successful son-in-law treated us to a five-star restaurant to celebrate our daughter's milestone birthday. The restaurant was lovely and certainly lived up to its reputation of a top-drawer dining arena in Colorado Springs. Our teenaged grandchildren joined us making it a party of six seated at a white linen covered, candle-lit round table. While viewing the leather-bound menu, I commented on the Sea Bass listed as one of the Chef's favorites.

"Oh, the Sea Bass is excellent here," our gracious host remarked with enthusiasm. As I recall, the Sea Bass selection was about $32, which cost less than the prime, long horn beefsteaks the rest of hungry crew wrangled up.

After a while, as highbrow as it could ever get, six waiters arrived, each carrying a presentation, which was covered by a large, silver dome. To add ambiance, each domed covered-plate was expertly placed in front of each recipient for added dining anticipation. I could hardly wait to see my sea bass presentation under the impressive dome. On cue, each waiter leaned over to lift a doom at the same, precise moment. I felt like the Queen of England until the dome was lifted. I nearly gasped. The Sea Bass resting in the center of my large plate was about the size of my big toe. I blinked but said nothing. I sheepishly glanced in the direction of my husband's Texas size steak as he lustily began slicing the tender, juicy, succulent meat. I graciously ate the sea bass and all the watercress surrounding it and filled up with bread. The only possible conclusion for that tiny portion was that perhaps the chef caught a glimpse of me strolling in and decided I needed to shed a few pounds.

A few seconds into the meal someone inquired, "How is your Sea Bass?"

"It was delicious!" If they had been listening carefully, my gracious past tense telltale clue revealed it had already been eaten in two bites. Now, I had honestly intended to take that disappointment to my grave until Bonnie's disappointing salmon confession jarred it loose from the recall vault.

# Childhood Survival of
# Mercury Contamination & Fried Everything!

My husband often comes out with the funniest remarks without trying to be comical. Last week I was broiling some flank steaks for dinner. Following her last college exam, our young family friend, Katrina, stopped over to eat dinner. I pulled the medium-rare steaks from the oven and continued cooking her portion for another 15 minutes. She won't touch meat that has a twinge of pink showing. Over the years, we've tried to get Katrina to eat steak medium well, to no avail. Dry, hard, over-cooked meat is the only way she likes it, drenched in hot sauce. She would have loved the '60s.

While waiting for her steak to continue broiling, the topic of beef cuts came up for discussion with Katrina. Ever the teacher, Daryl attempted to explain the differences in cost due to beef quality and yield grades. "Wow, I didn't know that," Katrina responded with an air of indifference. She would never taste the difference once costly prime meat was over cooked to resemble shoe leather.

"Well, when I grew up, we didn't eat steak," he explained. "We had hamburger patties four nights a week. My mother fried them to death. They were so black and hard that if you threw them at a window it would break." Katrina stared at me not knowing why I was doubled over with laughter because I had instant recall of the hamburger hockey pucks my mother also dished up from her trusty black, cast iron skillet.

By the time the top broiler was invented for the American oven our arteries were so clogged up it took decades to clear them out. But we survived.

Last night, at my weekly writer's group, Gayle looked over at me since we're the same age. She said, "Do you remember playing with mercury as a kid?"

"Yes!" I said with glee. "You could hold in your hand and poke at it to split off in little silver droplets that moved across the table, but wouldn't run off. I loved rubbing mercury on quarters to make them bright and shiny. My dad used to bring it home from the chemical plant he worked at."

Gayle chuckled. "Yeah, any time a thermometer broke in biology class we'd break our necks to scoop the puddle of mercury off the floor. Our whole class took turns playing with it. Last week an entire drug store shut down for three days because of a small mercury spill. The police were called in and the T.V. news channels warned everyone in the store that day to destroy their shoes in case they stepped in it."

Yep. We were a chosen generation all right. We've survived mercury contamination and grease-clogged arteries from decades of pan-fried foods. It's no wonder nothing seems to bother us!

# Old Habits Are Tough to Break

If our insurance agent knew my husband left the keys in his car each time he pulled into the garage for the night our rates would triple. To end the irritating, buzzing warning signal, Daryl pulls the keys from the ignition and plops them in the cup holder assuming an expert car thief wouldn't notice.

Last week my husband and I drove from Ohio to our new home in Cape Coral, Florida. It's a sixteen-hundred-mile trek and I'm getting old. We journeyed back with our remaining boxer, Peetie, who was a better backseat traveler than the two grouchy senior citizens seated up front.

We made it to the far end of Tennessee without incident. Fortunately, the weather was chilly when calamity happened in Sweetwater. Up until then all our timely pit stops had been routine. At each stop, I'd put the leash on Peetie and guide her to the nearest spot of grass. After she dutifully tinkled, I'd fill her traveling cup with water out of a plastic bottle and watch her lap down two inches of water. I'd secure her back in the empty car while my husband filled the gas tank or visited the men's room. Peetie never complained.

In some remote part of the country, we stopped for gas for the second fill-up on our three-tank trip home. Fortunately, the weather was a balmy 60 degrees. After securing Peetie in her back seat, I doubled checked to see if the keys were in the ignition before I hit the door lock.

Together, hubby and I moseyed around the convenient store aisles selecting a few snacks: cheddar popcorn (my favorite) and Daryl's Gatorade to eat with his favorite low fat cookies. The lady behind the counter gave us a friendly bid goodbye as we exited the store. As we neared the car, Daryl asked for the keys.

"You have the keys," I replied. No need to check because my purse was in the car, which was why I locked it.

"No, I don't. You have the keys."

"Well, you must have the keys. I checked the ignition before I locked the door."

Daryl walked over to the passenger side of the car. He loomed over to better see through the window. Suddenly, his body jerked up with a start. "You locked the keys in the car! They're in the cup holder!"

"Well, what on earth are they doing in the cup holder?"

We both considered the other a complete idiot but said nothing of the stupidity.

Daryl darted back into the store. He was talking to the nice lady behind the counter as I walked back into the store.

"Now, I suppose he's blaming me for locking the keys in the car." I actually sounded jolly. The situation was so bizarre I must have split from my true self momentarily.

"No, actually I was explaining to her what happened." He spoke in a controlled, third-grade Sunday school teacher voice. He, too, must have splintered off.

When my husband walked outside to make some phone

calls, she spoke with genuine sympathy. "I've locked my keys in my car."

Later, after responding to my text message about our situation, Bo, our adult son, wasn't as sympathetic. He quickly shot back a simple text: "Kidding me." He, too, thought we were complete idiots.

While munching my cheddar popcorn, I stood on the curb observing several cars whiz in and out for gas. It was a busy place and most customers had things to say about our situation. One Tennessee longhorn with a big truck commented with a chuckle. "Yeah, I thought I had done that same dumb thing last week, but I didn't."

In a near whisper, one concerned woman spoke guardedly. "Well, if you call the police and tell them a child or pet is in the car they will probably come right out."

If I only knew where we were I might do just that. Thankfully, it was not hot out. Otherwise, I would have been in a crazed dither over Peetie trapped in a heated car and my true self would have quickly manifested.

One blond lady with a Praise the Lord plate on her front bumper commented on my Boxer. "Oh, I miss mine so much!" she said with a sorrowful smile. I didn't dare tell her mine was locked in the car.

Within minutes my husband determined the nearest Toyota dealership was an hour and half south of our current location. He called the Michigan dealer/client who leased us the car and learned that we had emergency roadside assistance anywhere in the United States of America. Unfortunately, the nearest city was also an hour away.

In a desperate attempt to rectify the situation I attempted to coax Peetie to the front seat hoping she'd pounce her paws on the door locks and mash open the door. A previous dog had locked me out of my car by pressing paws on a door lock. I thought maybe it would work in reverse. It was worth a try. So, I merrily knocked on the passenger side window and spoke encouraging words to Peetie's curious face as she stared back, wagging her tail. Her front paws were perched on the console between the driver's seat and the passenger seat but she wouldn't hop through. After all, it was a new car. I got in front of the car knocking happily on the hood and waving and clapping to rile her up. However, no response, she, too, is getting old. I returned to the side window trying in vain to get her to move from her perch. Habits are hard to break. It was no wonder gas customers were readily making comments.

"Hey, let's go to the hotel right there and wait for the service man," I suggested. "There are probably some magazines to read." The lobby door was in full view of my car.

"No, I better not leave the car. I don't want to chance he arrives and we're not here." Even though the emergency roadside service agent asked for the make, model, serial number and color of my new, bright red Camry, and my car was within shouting distance from the hotel, Daryl was suddenly not taking any risks by leaving its side.

I sauntered over to the hotel thirty paces away. In the quiet lobby, a comfortable, brown leather sofa was waiting for me to relax and drink a free cup of coffee and read a complimentary newspaper. An hour later, the roadside assistance attendant came to our rescue at no charge. I thoroughly relaxed during the wait.

At any rate, all that fresh air probably did my husband's memory some good. However, just in case, the next time I see those magnetic "hidden key" storage boxes to plant under the bumper, I'm buying one for each car and several more for my same-age friends who travel by automobile. No sense in taking chances traveling with a senior set in his ways. Lifelong habits are sure tough to break.

# Kept in the Dark Too Long

Well, it happened again. By the time I frantically located my cell phone, it was on the rinse cycle. After the first time going through the wash, you'd think that horror could only happen once in a lifetime.

Yesterday, after asking my husband to call my flip-top phone from his Droid and not hearing it ring, I had a sinking feeling the wash cycle is where I'd find it.

The last time my cell phone was machine washed in Tide I placed it in rice. Eight days later I was able to turn the phone back on. That was a hallelujah moment because I had over 300 cell phone numbers stored. Within a week I could make calls. I continued using it for a few weeks before it gave up the ghost. The Verizon agent explained why. Once a cell phone gets wet it begins to corrode. At that point I begged him to try a new battery in to retrieve my phone contacts. It worked. After downloading all my phone numbers, he hooked me up to automatic cyberspace storage for any added contacts in case I ever lost my new cell phone. That was five years ago.

'Just put it in rice," my husband said nonchalantly from his relaxed reading position in our outdoor spa. He keeps his gorgeous Florida tan with a least an hour of sunshine daily. My pasty skin resembles an Alaskan native or someone exiting a deep cave.

"I am not waiting two weeks to use my phone," I snapped, starting to feel like a real live Neanderthal. My flip top cell phone is way behind the times. But at least I no longer have to text using the ABC method. Two years ago, my texting skills were catapulted by my free upgrade with an actual keyboard. I now use commas and capital letters with correct subject/verb agreement, so my text messages are clearly understood. My husband uses one to three word encoded text messages to decipher. It takes me longer to figure out what he's encrypted than it would if he just took the time to spell out the entire word. *P cms n @ 4* (Plane comes in at 4 pm). That text message took me about fifteen minutes to figure out.

One time I flew into the Ft. Myers airport late at night. Our boomerang son, Bo, was scheduled to be waiting on my arrival in the cell phone lot. However, when I texted if he was out there, his response was "Y" which meant, "yes" but I interpreted it as "why?" I thought he was being a smart aleck until my husband later explained. Is it really that difficult to spell out a simple three-letter utterance?

So, yesterday, the cell phone rinse cycle dilemma happened at 4:45pm and I promptly Googled to locate the nearest Verizon store in our community. It closed at 6pm.

Two weeks ago, I came home from an extended visit in Ohio to my Boxer infested with fleas. Daryl and Bo were in charge of the dog in my absence. They obviously missed the monthly topical flea treatment.

After the pesticide man sprayed down our home yesterday, we were instructed to keep the dog outside for an hour. An hour later, fully clothed, I stood in the shower with Ruby and scrubbed her down with flea & tick killer shampoo. After rinsing and patting her down with a towel, I quickly stripped my damp clothes off to wash with the infested towel used to dry her off. My cell phone was in the side pocket of my cotton Capri's.

Dealing with fleas put me in a foul disposition before the cell phone incident nearly sent me over the edge. So when I appeared on the patio in my flannel P.J.'s I wasn't the most diplomatic when announcing my ruined cell phone woes.

"I need your phone to call the Verizon store to see if they still carry this phone," I vented despairingly. I had no idea how to make a call from his "smart" phone, so my husband explained. Back inside the house, I managed to successfully place the call, but when the prompt recording asked me to "press three for customer service" there was no keyboard on the screen. Back I went out to the patio spa, but this time I was in near tears. Without a word, I calmly placed his "dumb" phone on the side of the spa and walked back into the house like a catatonic escapee from an insane asylum.

My dripping wet husband appeared moments later to place the urgent call to Verizon. He obviously recognized my near-the-brink warning signs. After going through numerous prompts he finally got a live salesman. "He is going to call me back because everyone is tied up with customers."

"Yeah?" I responded dubiously. "He'll probably call back at five minutes to six." I suggested we drive over and take our chances. I quickly changed out of my comfy pajamas to dart off before closing time.

"We don't even make that model anymore," said Verizon Jim, eyeing me with pity. Seated at his desk, he located our four-phone family account on his computer screen. He glanced up at my husband who remained standing. "For the same amount of money each month we can put her in a digital model."

My husband eyed him suspiciously and remained stoic. His high tech phone is used for business. Internet and email access is necessary, so the added $40 dollars a month is justified.

Jim seemed to read his mind. "You have never used your data downloading yet. And we can set it up so you're warned when you're close to your data limit."

Taking Daryl's silence as agreement, Jim quickly disappeared to retrieve the free upgrade phone choices. In his absence my husband voiced his apprehension. "Well," he grumbled, "they say there is not extra cost, but it's just like our cable network. You add an upgrade and there's always hidden costs added on each month on the bill."

Smiling demurely, I remained still.

Jim returned and addressed hubby's concerns after I voiced them. After tearing down every stronghold with facts, Daryl conceded that I could enter the digital age to match all my nieces, nephews and grandchildren whose faces are often glued to their jazzy, flat screen, high-tech cell phones.

Jim showed us the two options. "This is the phone I got my mother. It's a free upgrade and this other one is free after rebate and it's military grade. Both have Wi-Fi accessibility.

*Military grade?* Not wanting to rock the boat by spending upfront money, I selected the model Jim's dear mother owned. It wasn't likely I'd be in a war zone anytime soon.

"As a new user, I suggest you get a cover protector," Jim warned. "What's your favorite color?" he asked leading me to the phone cover selections on the wall.

"Purple?" I called out after him, grinning like a kid tagging along in a toy store.

"That's his favorite color, too!" That was a smart-aleck co-worker calling out to us.

I chose a hot pink cover since purple was not even offered. Back at his desk, Jim gingerly placed the plastic protector on the glass screen and uploaded all my stored phone contacts. I watched in gleeful anticipation.

While Jim hooked me up to the 21$^{st}$ Century, he commented, "My mom loves this phone because she could never text with her old phone. She'd write out her message on paper, take a picture of it and then send it to me. Now all she has to do is talk into the phone and it types out her messages. Now I get real long paragraphs from her."

"What?" I was flabbergasted. "I can speak my text messages? Are you kidding?"

"Yeah, and you can ask a question and it will give you the answer. Google makes this phone. Let's ask it a question."

The same wisecrack co-worker called out, "Ask 'who is Nicki Minaj's sister'?"

"Who is Nicki Minaj?" Jim asked, frowning.

Even I knew that answer. I watch American Idol and Nicki was a judge last year.

My husband was most likely calculating the monthly

data I'd use-up Face Booking, Googling silly questions and emailing all my friends from Starbucks. It's no wonder he kept me in the dark for so long. I guess I have to thank my dog for catching me up to the latest and greatest cell phone technology. Maybe I'll figure out how to trend on Twitter and Insta-Gram with my fabulous new pink phone. Thank you, Ruby, my darling dog—I owe you one!

# An Afterword

*This is our tribute to Barbara from your greatest fans and the two characters most featured in this book—Your husband Daryl and closest friend, Susan Furci. With Susan's prompting, I submitted this story to the author to see if I could squeeze in the last word—for the first time and probably the last time!*

From Daryl's pen:

Barbara is unique—as in one of a kind. Her energy and spirit is what attracted me in the first place. She cares for others like no one I know. When she gets someone in her sights, look out, for she won't let go. She has been criticized for holding on to others when everyone else gave up. But that's my Barbara— like it or not.

When I met Barbara she was twenty-three years old. I was twenty-eight and divorced for about six months before meeting her. I had played for the NFL, but she never knew me as an offensive tackle. At the time, I was an executive VP of a Fortune 500 company, so all she knew was I floated in "high circles." I was using the company jet, flying to Europe often, spending frequent weekends in New York City, but also a concerned father who flew into Detroit every few weeks to visit my two children. She lived in Dearborn, so whenever I visited my ten and eleven-year-old kids, I also spent meaningful time with Barbara.

While we dated we attended several Detroit Lions games to watch my old teammates play. She had no clue as to what was happening on the field – and no interest in the details. We usually went with a player's girlfriend, so the girls would yak throughout the game paying little attention to what was happening out on the field.

At that time, my residence was Dayton, Ohio enabling us to attend many Ohio State games with friends in the seats I have had for over forty years. At the postgame festivities, Barbara was always the life of the party. She also became the official designated driver since she never drank. These were our days we called "BC." That is "Before Christ" came into our lives. We all partied away with sober Barbara instigating the songs and fun.

On OSU football Saturdays, Barbara rated the countless pre-game tailgate parties by the crowd size, food selection and overall game-day enthusiasm. She reminded me that her highest rating went to a huge parking lot party featuring an upright piano hauled in on a pickup truck planted next to a giant keg of beer. She loved the stadium atmosphere, but she probably still doesn't know what's required for a first down. I've always reasoned that her lack of interest in my former football career is because she was a sophomore in high school when I was a rookie for the Detroit Lions. After my retirement from football, Barbara met a dignified, well-dressed businessman, so she couldn't imagine me wearing a football uniform. Perhaps my stoic demeanor seemed contrary to an offensive tackle running and hitting others, although many players are just as stoic, but she's had no reference point.

Writing this, forty-years later, I just spent a bittersweet OSU football weekend in Columbus, Ohio. I went back to attend my team's 50th reunion of our National Championship team. Barbara stayed in Florida to care for her recently widowed and handicapped mother who has moved in with us.

Ironically, Barbara's best friend is a football fanatic and Susan prompted me to get in the last word since "our little talebearer" has certainly had a "field day" telling stories on us

Whenever Susan is in their Venice, Florida winter home on game day, she'll often go to a sports bar, alone, to watch the Bucks play. Now that's a true fan! But Susan has never met a stranger in an elevator, so she's always links up with fellow Buckeye fans to form a happy tailgate party of her own.

Our friendship with Dr. Don and Susan Furci spans thirty-five years. We raised our children together and have shared many of life's up and downs in this journey called life. As an avid sports fan, Susan knows all of the nuances of a football game. She still can't grasp Barbara's fundamental lack of interest in football, so she'll often text me in the middle of a game.

The latest football incident happened while I was in a stadium box at the Ohio State homecoming game last weekend. Susan was in Venice without Don. Barbara was home in Cape Coral.

Susan texted me and did not get a response (too much noise in the box).

Later, I read Susan's text. She wrote: "It states with me texting u 2 see if you are at the game. When I don't hear from u I call B and leave a message. A few minutes later I get the first text. Here goes:

Barbara: "He is at the game-was MC for dinner last nite."

Susan: "R u watcin the game?  How r u doing?  (This is me being compassionate, regarding her mom)

Barbara: "What channel?  We are Comcast"

Susan: "29 espn sports"

Barbara: (9:01 pm) "Got it"

Barbara: (9:11 pm) "Did they half time yet?  (Note she has had it on for 10 minutes…does she not realize that the score and time are on the TV screen?  Too funny!)

Susan: (9:12pm) "Not yet, u r just in time.  A few more minutes 2:13 seconds"

Barbara: "Is it really necessary for nine to pile on one player??" (At this point I just roared!"

Susan: "You r sooo funny! have u every watched an entire game? or dare say enjoyed one?"

Barbara: (9:25pm) "N-O! You are the star of my memoir I need to send u some copies! I found a dedication page mistake. A friend's name misspelled, so I need to update the file – process will take a few weeks."

*We text back and forth for 25 more minutes regarding Barbara's home care of her feisty Mother.*

Barbara: NURSE RATCHED IS FINE!

Barbara: (9:50pm) "GO BUCKS!"

Susan: "They look pretty good, 2 bad we missed half time with the gray ghost". (too many commercials)

Barbara: "Who r u with? Is Doc reading the bible?"

Susan: "That's funny! I am home alone in my pj's watching the game"

(End of text messages between Susan and Barbara)

\*     \*     \*

From Daryl's pen:

I had been in Columbus for a football reunion at OSU. I arrived home last Monday evening. On the ride back from the airport Barbara inquired about my reunion weekend.

She said, "Hey, did OSU win the game? I forget—who did they play?"

"Yes, we beat Wisconsin."

"Well, I turned on the game in time for halftime but ESPN didn't show it. So, did they honor your team on the field at half time?"

"Not really," I said with a tone of disgust. "OSU and NIKE used our 1961 National Championship Team as a promotional hook to advance the sales of their 'Throw-back jerseys,' but they sure didn't spring for dinner or give us much attention at half time.

"Really? That's too bad…what happened?"

"At halftime the announcer called out the individual names of about twenty faculty members for some vague award as they herded out team way into the end zone. By then the two teams came running back on the field to warm up by kicking balls into both end zones. The announcer roared 'Welcome members of the 1961 championship game,' so we got our fifteen seconds of fame and glory while dodging balls."

Barbara burst out laughing.

I'm smiling, too, because as I reflect on my now obscure football career, it was ridiculous to be out on the field as a bunch of white haired former players, especially to be regarded as has-beens.

But it was sure great to mingle among my old teammates and reminisce about two of the greatest top-ten college coaches of all time: Woody Hayes and Bo Schembechler, who coached our championship team. It was a privilege to play for them and an honor to represent Ohio State University.

One legendary halftime story that none of my teammates will never forget was a home game against Oregon when we were losing 12 to 7. In the locker room there was a blackboard on wheels about four feet by six feet and waist high in size. Woody was at the blackboard going over every disappointing play while smashing the chalk on the board to emphasize that we needed to "hit somebody for a change" in the second half.

Woody got so enraged that he threw the rest of the chalk across the room. He was left handed and turned on the board to deliver another blow but his fist went through the blackboard instead. He started to jerk his hand back but it was stuck! He was yelling and cussing but could not pull out his fist. Our team stifled the urge to burst out laughing, which required every ounce of the discipline Woody had ever instilled in us. Finally, after continuing to struggle to free his fist he yelled, "Well! Get out there and hit somebody!"

We won the game 22-12. The next day a dozen of us located the infamous blackboard in the trash bin under the stadium. We each took turns punching the board but not one of us could slam our fist through it!

So, my dear Barbara, I really don't mind your lack of interest in football. After all, the game is really just about people and friends and memories, which we have spent a lifetime sharing.

I adore you and so do all your loving fans.

# Acknowledgments

Published authors owe a huge debt of gratitude to all the spare eyes that proof read, edit, critique, and encourage.

I appreciate my circle of writer friends who challenge and inspire me to keep writing when most of my other pals are off playing golf or enjoying a paid vacation. But I wouldn't have it any other way. I didn't start writing until my kids were grown, so now, "during retirement," I have something worth writing about because I've lived an exciting life with no regrets.

On every publication, thank you, always, to the late Ms. Grace T. Blakely, Northern Michigan University, you were my encouraging English professor who was the first to call me a writer.

Thank you, Mr. Frank Deaner, executive director of the Ohio News Association. After reading a few of these stories, you were the first to boost my confidence, which inspired me to keep writing more of these vignettes.

Thank you, Dr. Dennis Hensley, associate professor of English at Taylor University. My ability to make you laugh was true inspiration beyond words.

Thank you, Ella Coleman, founder of *Purpose* magazine, Columbus, Ohio. Publishing my more serious articles in your magazine has been a confidence boost, too.

Thank you to Kelly Tompkies, founder of Christian Family Magazine, Columbus, Ohio. Your encouragement is always appreciated, too.

Thank you, kind friend, Renny Severance, for your tireless efforts to format and edit with such gracious devotion when you could be playing golf during retirement from your newspaper publication!

My Columbus writing group and current Cape Coral critique group offer fellowship with other authors who share my passion for writing.

Blessings to Linda Rice (Columbus) for giving this book a final read and to Patty Duncan (Cape Coral) for a read through the additional chapters I wrote since arriving in Florida! May you both know how much I value your editorial input!

While living in Columbus, every Tuesday night, I met with fellow fiction writers, Julia Blaine, Julie Glista, Gayle Heston, Linda Rice, and Lori Snow for an early dinner followed by several hours at Borders bookstore.

Tragically, our Lori passed away in August 2010. My friend was a spark of sunshine to all of us in the writing group. Her sudden diabetes-related death deeply saddened us because she was a young woman who died long before her time. She was a very gifted writer. She certainly made a rich deposit of kindness in our lives!

So, dear Lori, may the love of your life, five-year-old nephew, Bailey, your precious little companion, who you inspired to love books, always remember how much you adored spending creative time with him.

Lori, I appreciated your phone call after you read *The Laborers Are Few*. You marveled how that, in faith, Alex Leonovich, broadcasted the Gospel of Jesus Christ in his native Russian language. For years, in America, he produced teaching tapes to broadcast to a vast continent not knowing if he was actually being heard on Radio Free Europe. You asked if my ears were burning because you had told all your friends about this amazing testimony. With much enthusiasm you announced, "I'll be at your first book signing!" I know you'll be right beside me in spirit. May *The Laborers Are Few* be an encouragement to your large Vermont family who is grieving the loss of a faithful daughter, sister and a loving and generous aunt. All of us who knew and loved Lori share their loss, too.

Without losing a beat, I've joined an equally fun writers group here in Cape Coral! Thank you, Dr. John Domino, for your enthusiasm and ability to encourage so many writers to join you at The Landings for terrific and beneficial round table fellowship. Blessings to every dedicated artist in the group who desires to write and glorify the Lord! May we continue to encourage one another is our desire to perfect the craft and learn from each other.

God bless you all!

# About the Author

Barbara Taylor Sanders, B.A., is a versatile author of fiction and non-fiction.

As an event planner and volunteer advocate for the poor and disadvantaged, she's shared the platform with Mrs. Coretta Scott King, Dr. Billy Graham, Elizabeth Dole, Johnny Cash, Pat Robertson, and best-selling authors: Evelyn Christenson, and Ann Kiemel Anderson to name a few. Barbara has been a featured testimony on *The 700 Club* viewed around the world.

She's the past president of the Columbus Christian Writers Association and has had numerous Christian magazine articles published.

Barbara has addressed university postgraduate students and conducted writing workshops at conferences and the Cape Coral Art Studio. She's a board member of the National League of American Pen Women of SW Florida.

All her books are listed online: *Puttin' On the Dog & Gettin' Bit* (humor) and novels; *Bloodline Secrets, The Bloodstone Ring,* (historical fiction) Her non-fiction books include; *The Laborers Are Few,* and *Holy Spirit: For Real.*

Barbara is married to author/lecturer, Daryl Sanders, a former star offensive tackle at Ohio State University under Coach Woody Hayes and a number one draft pick for the NFL. As longtime community leaders in Columbus, Ohio, the Sanders now reside in Cape Coral, Florida.

For conference scheduling to invite Barbara to speak, please contact her at barbarataylorsanders@comcast.net.

## Inspirational Books for Seminars and Bible Studies

### *A Heart After God*

(Developing A Prayer Language

From the Book of Psalms)

*

### *Exploring Avenues of Prayer*

(A Look at The Prayers of Apostle Paul)

*

### *Becoming a Woman of Influence*

(Using Our God-Given Position of Appeal)

*

### *Parting the Waters*

(Stepping Out in Faith for The Promise)

*

### *Knowing the Voice of God*

(Discernment by Reason of Use)

### *Listening Heart*

(Developing an Obedient Attitude)

\*

### Taking Your Stand

(Putting On the Full Armor of God)

\*

### Capturing Strongholds

(Taking Authority Over Wrong Thoughts)

\*

### Loving Your Enemies

(Learning Forbearance Through Forgiveness)

\*

### Free to Love

(Conquering Bitterness)

\*

### Justified by Faith

(Overcoming Dead Works)

\*

### Governed by Grace

(Empowered for Right Choices)


### Expressions of Praise

(Spiritual Warfare, Part 1)

\*

*Expressions of Worship*

(Spiritual Warfare, Part 2)

\*

*Expressing God to Others*

(Creative Ways to Reach the Lost)

\*

*Becoming a Sweet Fragrance*

(Becoming a Broken Vessel)

\*

*Risen Indeed*

(Resurrection Power Over Everything)

\*

*Rising Above Circumstances*

(Transforming Irritations into Victories)

\*

*Loving Kindness*

(Putting on Bowels of Mercy)


*Gracious Endeavors*

(Extending Our Hands to the Poor and Disadvantaged)

\*

## Running the Race

(Developing Endurance)

\*

## Famous Last Words

(Encouragement from the Apostle Paul to Timothy)

\*

## Jumping for Joy

(Healthy Responses to Difficulties)

\*

## Released in the Spirit

(Prophesying to the Dead Bones)

\*

## Captured by Love

(A life Not My Own)

\*

## Time is Running Out

(Praying for the Lost)

Made in the USA
Columbia, SC
19 January 2019